Faith
Words

LARGE
PRINT

OVERLOAD

How to Unplug, Unwind, and Unleash
Yourself from the Pressure of Stress

JOYCE MEYER

Faith
Words

LARGE PRINT

Unless otherwise noted Scriptures are taken from *The Amplified Bible* (AMP). *The Amplified Bible*, Old Testament, copyright © 1965, 1987 by The Zondervan Corporation. *The Amplified New Testament*, copyright © 1954, 1958, 1987 by The Lockman Foundation. Used by permission.

Scriptures noted (NIV) are taken from the *Holy Bible: New International Version* ®. Copyright © 1973, 1978, 1984 by International Bible Society. Used by permission of Zondervan Publishing House. All rights reserved.

Scripture quotations marked (KJV) are taken from the King James Version of the Bible.

Scripture quotations marked (NLT) are taken from the *Holy Bible*, New Living Translation, Copyright © 1996. Used by permission of Tyndale House Publishers, Inc., Wheaton, Illinois 60189. All rights reserved.

FaithWords
Hachette Book Group
1290 Avenue of the Americas
New York, NY 10104

www.faithwords.com

Printed in the United States of America

RRD-C

First Edition: March 2016

10 9 8 7 6 5 4 3 2 1

FaithWords is a division of Hachette Book Group, Inc.

The FaithWords name and logo are trademarks of Hachette Book Group, Inc.

The Hachette Speakers Bureau provides a wide range of authors for speaking events. To find out more, go to www.hachettespeakersbureau.com or call (866) 376-6591.

The publisher is not responsible for websites (or their content) that are not owned by the publisher.

Library of Congress Cataloging-in-Publication Data

Names: Meyer, Joyce, 1943–
Title: Overload : how to unplug, unwind, and unleash yourself from the pressure of stress / Joyce Meyer.
Description: First [edition]. | New York : Faith Words, 2016. | Includes bibliographical references.
Identifiers: LCCN 2015039434 | ISBN 9781455559831 (hardcover) | ISBN 9781455559848 (large-print hardcover) | ISBN 9781455559855 (Spanish language trade pbk.) | ISBN 9781478985082 (audio download) | ISBN 9781478985099 (audio cd) | ISBN 9781455559862 (ebook)
Subjects: LCSH: Stress (Psychology)—Religious aspects—Christianity. | Stress management—Religious aspects—Christianity.
Classification: LCC BV4509.5 .M4755 2016 | DDC 248.8/6—dc23 LC record available at http://lccn.loc.gov/2015039434

ISBN 978-1-4555-5983-1 (hardcover)
ISBN 978-1-4555-5984-8 (large print)
ISBN 978-1-4555-6625-9 (international trade)

CONTENTS

Anxiety in a man's heart weighs it down, but an encouraging word makes it glad.

Proverbs 12:25

INTRODUCTION

Wow! I am so excited about this book. I have a great expectation that it will truly help you learn how to manage and even eliminate the stress in your life. Let me tell you why I have a special excitement about *Overload: How to Unplug, Unwind, and Unleash Yourself from the Pressure of Stress.*

In my years of ministry, I've taught and written on a wide variety of topics. *Knowing God Intimately, The Power of Your Words, Obeying God's Voice, Overcoming Fear, Living with Hope, The Battlefield of the Mind, Receiving God's Love, Enjoying Your Life*—just to name a few.

And while each topic that God has led me to write or teach about is important, I feel like there's something particularly significant about this book. You see, *stress* is a subject I'm all too familiar with. This isn't just an issue I've studied. It's not a theme I've merely read about. And it's not a topic I've only witnessed from a distance.

Stress is something I've had to deal with.

It's a nagging enemy I've battled. Sometimes

winning and sometimes losing, stress is an adversary I've dealt with in the past…and something I still need to confront and resist in my life today.

There have been many days when stress has tried to steal my peace and hijack my joy. Hectic circumstances, busy schedules, and poor choices have been the entryway through which stress has come barging in. And I do mean *barging in*. Stress rarely sneaks into our lives through a back alley. It prefers to come rushing through the front door.

You may be able to relate to what I am saying. As a matter of fact, I have a feeling you know *exactly* what I'm talking about. I'm sure you've dealt with your share of frustrations, pressures, and stressful situations. You've probably had days when the bills piled up, the kids drove you crazy, the boss seemed unreasonable, and the car started making that funny noise again. (You may be having one of those days today.)

So, it looks like you and I are in the same boat. You may not know all the specifics (though I'll share some of them with you in the pages to come), but you can relate to the stress I have experienced. And I may not know all the specifics, but I can relate to yours.

I think that's why I'm so excited to be writing this book, and I'm equally excited you're reading it. I feel like we're in this together. You and I—we're fellow sojourners on this journey to reduce our stress levels. We've both felt exasperated, we've both been discouraged, and we've both contemplated escaping to a beach somewhere so everyone will leave us alone. (Just kidding...kind of.)

But let me zoom the camera out wider than just you and me. There's a bigger picture here I want you to see. Did you know there is someone else who understands the pressures of stress? Someone else who can identify with what you're going through when life gets crazy and things get out of control?

That person is Jesus.

If that answer surprises you, consider for a moment some of the stressors I believe Jesus faced:

1. His ragtag group of disciples needed correction on a regular basis.
2. The Pharisees and the Sadducees constantly tried to publically discredit His ministry.
3. Huge crowds formed everywhere He went, begging for miracles.
4. The people in His own hometown of Nazareth rejected His teaching.
5. One of His chosen followers betrayed Him for thirty pieces of silver.

Sounds pretty stressful to me. And that doesn't even take into consideration the fact that Jesus was on a divine mission to save humanity from our sins and reconnect us to God. Jesus knew He was going to die a cruel death; it was no surprise to Him. Yet He never stopped marching toward the cross. That's a stress that none of us can ever imagine. It may be difficult to remember that Jesus experienced stress, but the Bible teaches us that He understands all of our weaknesses and infirmities because He was tempted in all respects just as we are, yet He never sinned (Hebrews 4:15).

But in the midst of all the stress and all the pressure, Jesus said things like:

> ***Peace I leave with you****; My [own] peace I now give and bequeath to you.*
>
> John 14:27 (emphasis added)

> *In the world you have…distress and frustration; but **be of good cheer** [take courage; be confident, certain, undaunted]! For I have overcome the world.*
>
> John 16:33 (emphasis added)

> *I have told you these things, that **My joy and delight may be in you**, and that your joy and gladness may be of full measure and complete and overflowing.*
>
> John 15:11 (emphasis added)

Also, in the midst of a hurricane-type storm, He rebuked the wind and told it to be still, and then He said to His disciples...

Why are you so timid and fearful? How is it that you have no faith (no firmly relying trust)?

Mark 4:40

Isn't that amazing? Despite the inconveniences, the challenges, and the pressures all around Him, Jesus remained peaceful and at rest. He went about the work before Him with confidence and joy, even as others were panicking and losing their cool.

No matter the circumstance—whether it was an unexpected storm or an angry mob—Jesus was a calming, steadying presence. This is why He could say in Matthew 11:28, "Come to Me, all you who labor and are heavy-laden and overburdened, and I will cause you to rest."

Jesus is still speaking those words—"Come to Me, and I will cause you to rest"—today. The life He wants you to live is not a life overrun by stress. You weren't meant to go through each day worried, anxious, and afraid, just waiting for the hammer to fall or the other shoe to drop. You can take all that stress, all that pressure, and learn to give it to God and live in the peace and the joy He has planned for your life.

I know that's true because I've seen it happen in my own life. I was faced with a choice years ago: I could give in to the stress and anxiety that I was feeling, or I could learn to follow the leading of the Holy Spirit and cast every care upon God.

When I began to trust God with my life, and as I began to really study and understand the effect stress and worry were having on me (spirit, soul, and body), I was amazed at the turnaround that began to take place. A transformation started to unfold in my life as I chose to make God-directed, daily decisions to overcome stress.

Sure, I still face the same stressors I always have. And, yes, there are still days that are more stressful than others. But my life is no longer overloaded with what Jesus called the "cares and anxieties of the world" (see Mark 4:19). Now when I'm faced with a situation that used to absolutely drive me bananas, by the grace of God, I've learned to keep my joy, trust God, and keep moving forward.

That's why I decided to write this book. I can't wait to show you what the Lord has taught me—and what He is *still* teaching me—about overcoming stress. No matter what you're facing—big or small, annoying or terrifying—believe me when I tell you: You don't have to live an anxious, worried, stressed-out life.

Trust me, I understand that you're dealing with

challenges and difficulties, sometimes on a daily basis. I know it can be exhausting trying to successfully navigate the stormy waters of life. But I want to encourage you today—you don't have to navigate those waters alone. God has promised that He is with you and that He will never leave your side (see Deuteronomy 31:6). And if God is with you, there is no problem, no debt, no trial, and no obstacle worth stressing out about. God's not going to let you sink. He is in control, and He is going to see you safely through to the other side.

Is your bank account running on empty?
Don't stress out. God is in control!

Do you have a big decision to make for your future?
Don't stress out. God is in control!

Is your marriage going through a difficult struggle?
Don't stress out. God is in control!

Has your doctor ordered more tests?
Don't stress out. God is in control!

Is there a new opportunity you've been hesitant to go after?
Don't stress out. God is in control!

*   *   *

That is what this book is all about. There will always be stressful situations we face, but with God's help, we're going to discover how to overcome that stress and learn to live the joy-filled, abundant life Jesus died to give us.

So, get ready. I believe God has something good in store. In the pages to come, I'll share my story and others. We'll talk about God's promises and His instruction. I'll give you some very practical and powerful steps to take. And through it all, in every chapter and on every page, I pray that you begin to see that stress is something you don't have to be overloaded with any longer—stress is something you can overcome!

OVERLOAD

KEEP
CALM
AND
DE-STRESS

CHAPTER 1

Start Defeating Stress Today

Anxiety does not empty tomorrow of its sorrows,
but only empties today of its strength.
　　　　　　　　　　　　　—Charles Spurgeon

Stress. It's a word none of us really likes but we've all come to accept. The unfortunate but undeniable fact is that you and I live in a stress-filled world. Student or teacher, stay-at-home mom or working professional, living in the country or residing in a city—stress seems to find us all.

I came across one article that said stress is the new normal. And I guess for many people that's true. You don't have to look very far to find the evidence of that. We've all known friends or coworkers who suffer from "stress headaches." Drug companies produce numerous stress-reducing medicines. Retail stores make a fortune selling "stress balls." Physicians, websites, and employers offer a variety of "stress tests." Stress is like a virus that just keeps spreading.

Many people have contracted the stress virus…but they don't seem to realize it. Their friends and family see it. Their bosses and coworkers see it. Everyone around them knows that they're stressed out, but they're oblivious to it. They have not learned to recognize the symptoms of stress. They're going about each day anxious, upset, worried, tense, and frustrated, and they've just accepted this as a part of life. It's their "new normal."

Many people have contracted the stress virus... but they don't seem to realize it.

This certainly was the case for me. In the early years of my ministry, I was highly stressed, but I didn't know it. There were a number of contributing factors to my stress—the ministry was growing quickly, which kept me extremely busy; I wasn't resting or getting the proper nutrition; I overfilled my calendar because I didn't want to tell anyone no; I was still dealing with the emotional repercussions of having been abused by my father throughout my childhood; and in the midst of all the busyness, my husband Dave and I were raising four children. And...did I mention I was in the midst of the change of life and could not take any hormone therapy because of having had breast cancer?! Wow! Now I look at all of this and can fully understand why I was stressed out all the time, but amazingly I didn't recognize the symptoms.

With all the anxiety and frustration and running around, I just assumed this was how I was supposed to live. Stress became my new normal.

Because of my personality and work ethic, I didn't take the time to slow down and learn to prioritize my calendar or care for myself. I had a hundred plates spinning at once, and I was determined to not let any of them fall. The result of my well-intentioned but stubborn refusal to slow down was physical and emotional exhaustion. My body started breaking down, and I would cry at the drop of a hat.

Finally, I went to see a doctor. I was sure he could simply give me some medicine to get me back on my feet again so I could continue meeting all the demands I was putting on myself. I'll never forget what he told me: "Joyce, your physical and emotional problems are a result of stress. I think you need to make some changes."

This infuriated me. *Stress? I'm not stressed! I'm just busy!* It really bothered me that he would suggest I was stressed out. I thought I was too strong for stress. And I was convinced I was in God's will and, therefore, He wouldn't let me feel the bad effects of stress. After all, I had dedicated my life to serving God; how could I be suffering from stress? Looking for a different answer, I consulted another doctor, but he told me the same thing. No matter how many appointments I made, and no matter how many doctors I talked to, the answer was consistent and firm: "Joyce, you're stressed out." The last doctor suggested

> I thought I was too strong for stress.

I see a psychiatrist, and that really made me mad! My mother had suffered with mental illness, and I think in the back of my mind I was convinced if I admitted I was experiencing stress, I might somehow be headed in the same direction she had ended up in.

Things were a little different back then. Information wasn't as readily available as it is today, and not as much study had been done in regards to the harmful effects of stress. I think this is why I was hesitant to believe how much damage stress was bringing to my life. At the time, it was a total shock to me that stress could be the root cause of so many of the issues I was facing.

Here I was, serving God and doing what I knew He had called me to do, but I wasn't really enjoying my life. Rather than celebrating the opportunities God was giving me to teach His Word (what I love to do), stress had me in bondage. I was easily frustrated, I had aches and pains, I wasn't sleeping well, I was argumentative—the list goes on and on.

But I began to read about stress, and with the Lord's help, I finally began to see that the doctors were right. Stress was hurting me physically and emotionally. But the Lord also began to show me that stress was hurting me spiritually. I was allowing the external pressures of my life to affect my internal peace and joy. If I didn't make some major changes, I was never going to fully enjoy the life Jesus died to give me.

The Effects of Stress

The more people I've talked to over the years, the more I've come to realize that my story isn't that uncommon. As I share with friends and ministry partners how stressed and overwhelmed I felt at times, I'm usually met with understanding nods and I-know-exactly-what-you-mean reassurances. People from all walks of life have told me that at some point they, too, had to face the cold, hard truth that stress was keeping them from really living their best life.

Stress is an indiscriminate thief. It will take whatever it can from whomever it can. Health, peace, rest,

Health, peace, rest, relationships, laughter— stress wants to take it all.

relationships, laughter—stress wants to take it all. And like any thief, we can't deal with it until we realize it is out there, lurking in the shadows. If we don't know we're at risk, how can we protect ourselves?

Let me share some eye-opening statistics with you from recent studies and surveys:

- 49 percent of people surveyed said they have had a "major stressful event or experience" in the last year.[1]
- 83 percent of Americans are stressed out on the job.[2]

- 69 percent of people with high stress say their stress actually *increased* in the past year.[3]
- 41 percent of adults who are married say that they lost patience or yelled at their spouse due to stress in the past month.[4]
- 52 percent of those aged 18 to 33 years report that stress has kept them awake at night at least once in the past month.[5]

Stress, pressure, and anxiety are being reported by people all over the world at an alarming rate. There are studies too numerous to count that show we are a society overrun with stress. And this stress we face is having an alarming effect on the way we feel and act each day. Look at some of the effects the Mayo Clinic says stress has on us:[6]

Physical effects

- Headaches
- Muscle tension or pain
- Fatigue
- Change in sex drive
- Upset stomach

Emotional effects

- Anxiety
- Restlessness

- Lack of motivation
- Irritability or anger
- Sadness or depression

Behavioral effects

- Overeating
- Angry outbursts
- Drug or alcohol abuse
- Tobacco use
- Social withdrawal

And as bad as those effects are, they aren't even the most dangerous effects of stress. The National Institute of Mental Health says that "the continued strain on your body from routine stress may lead to serious health problems, such as heart disease, high blood pressure, diabetes, depression, anxiety disorder, and other illnesses."[7]

We can't close our eyes any longer. Stress is a real enemy, capable of doing real physical, emotional, and spiritual damage. It's not something to be trivialized and swept under the rug. Stress isn't just being "overly busy" or "a little nervous." Stress is a dangerous tool the enemy uses to try and keep us from enjoying the life Jesus died to give us.

What About You?

So far in this chapter, I've told you about the stress I was under—a stress that was holding me back even though I didn't realize it at the time. And I've told you about friends of mine who could relate because they had been through stress, too. Now I want to ask you about your life.

You see, I'm wondering if you're really experiencing and enjoying the best God has for you. I say that because I meet so many people who are worn down and worn out. It seems they're always tired, always upset, and always wishing for something better. No matter how hard they try, they just can't quite seem to pinpoint why they aren't happy. Sure, they have their good days, but if they're completely honest, they'll tell you that the bad days outnumber the good.

And it's not always about circumstances. Some of the most frustrated, unhappy people I know have all they've ever asked for—a loving spouse, beautiful children, a successful career, a great house. But even with all these things, they can't seem to find peace and celebrate life. There's no time for that. Instead, their days are filled with worry, nervousness, and uncertainty about the future.

Do you know that feeling? Have you felt unsettled or discontented recently? What about those symptoms from the Mayo Clinic? Headaches, pain, fatigue, restlessness, lack of motivation, irritability, anger, sadness, overeating, social withdrawal—have you dealt with any of these lately? If so, it's quite possible that you're dealing with stress (whether you know it or not). And stress is trying to rob you of the good things God has in store for your life.

Let me encourage you: The stress you're facing doesn't mean there is something wrong with you. As a matter of fact, it just means you're human. As the statistics show, men and women all around the world are feeling stress. But there is good news for us today—we don't have to live like the rest of the world. As believers, we have been promised a new life in Christ. We don't have to let stress rob us of our happiness. We don't have to sit back and think, *Oh well, I guess this is as good as it gets.* We can stand on the promises of God and trust that He is working out His great plan for our lives (more on this in the next chapter).

> God has a better life in store. A life full of laughter, contentment, provision, peace, and joy.

So, if you've ever wondered, *Is this as good as it gets?* the answer is a resounding no! God has a better life in store. A life full of laughter, contentment, provision, peace, and joy. But an important part of realizing all that God has for you is choosing to de-stress. Let me give you some simple steps to start that process.

5 Ways to De-Stress

Once you realize that stress is trying to keep you from experiencing God's best in your life, you can start making some necessary choices to change things. We're going to talk about those choices all throughout this book, but I want to give you some practical things right away in this first chapter so you can begin taking some initial steps today.

When you get a new phone or piece of electronic equipment, the manufacturer usually includes a "Get Started" card at the front of the instruction manual. Well, that's kind of what this is. Here are some steps you can take today to "get started" on overcoming stress:

1. Seek Out Social Support
   Studies show that isolation leads to elevated stress levels. As social beings, spending time with others is one of the best ways to improve our outlook. There are different social outlets that work better for different people; here are a few suggestions:
   □ **Family:** Spend time with family members who love and support you. Don't take them for granted.
   □ **Church:** The local church is where the family of God gathers to worship Him, learn

His Word, and encourage one another. If you're not in a strong, Bible-based church, I encourage you to find one to attend.

☐ **Groups and clubs:** Social groups of all kinds—book clubs, walking groups, Bible study groups, even groups of friends that simply meet for dinner once a week—are all shown to reduce stress.

☐ **Counseling:** If you don't have anyone else to talk to, being able to process emotions with a counselor can be a tremendous help in reducing stress and increasing overall emotional health. My suggestion would be to make sure it is someone who is well grounded in God's Word so the Holy Spirit, who is "the Counselor," leads the advice they give you.

2. Practice "Shrug Therapy"
   There are some things in life you can control— what job you take, what friends you spend time with, how much coffee you drink, and what time you go to bed. But there are other things you can't control—what other people say or do, fluctuations in the economy, that rude driver on the freeway.

   How you react to things you can't control will many times determine your stress level.

People who regularly get upset over small things are easily frustrated and highly stressed. People who shrug those things off are much happier.

People who regularly get upset over small things are easily frustrated and highly stressed. People who shrug those things off are much happier.

Shrugging doesn't mean you're indifferent or don't care about what is happening around you; it simply means you're acknowledging there is nothing you can do at that moment to change the situation. The best approach when things are beyond your control is to shrug it off and trust God to work things out for your good (see Romans 8:28).

3. Find Your Comfort Zone... and Stay There

My husband, Dave, once did one of the wisest things I've seen. When he was working as an engineer, he was offered a promotion that came with a big pay raise and a lot of prestige. But he turned it down. At first I thought he was making a big mistake. *Couldn't we use the money? Didn't he want people in his company to look up to him?*

When I asked him about it, Dave told me that he had watched the other men who had previously been in that position. He said they traveled extensively, and they were constantly given unreasonable deadlines that put them under tremendous stress. He told me, "Joyce, that's not the way I want to live." Instead, he chose a position that allowed him to stick to his core values—commitment to family and comfort with self—rather than chasing what other people were chasing.

I'm convinced there would be much more happiness and less stress in the world if people would take the time to know themselves and their comfort zone and stay there. This extends beyond the workplace. If you are involved with something that is stealing your joy or your health, that is not your comfort zone—get out of there as quickly as you can. Removing all the things from your schedule that aren't bearing good fruit will greatly reduce your stress level and enable you to enjoy the things you choose to focus on.

4. Nutrition, Proven Supplements, Healthy Diet, and Exercise
What you put in your body has a huge impact on your stress level. Proper nutrition, proven supplements, and an overall healthy diet are major influences on how you feel each day.

I encourage you to thoughtfully put together a well-balanced, sensible combination of nutritious food and healthy, proven supplements and vita-mins in order to help offset daily stress.

I cannot state strongly enough the need for regular exercise. Many people think they don't have time to exercise, but the truth is if you don't take the time now, you may lose more time visiting doctors and having to be inactive and unproductive because you feel bad. Exercise is one of the best sources of energy you can find!

5. Schedule Time to Relax
Relaxation is not selfish or lazy. It is not slack-ing off. It's a way of recharging your batteries—physical, emotional, and spiritual—so that you can charge back into the fray at full strength the next day. You will get much more accom-plished and live longer and healthier if you'll take the time to treat yourself right.

There are thousands of ways you can relax. Whether it's unwinding with music, reading a good book, taking a warm bath by candle-light, going for a walk, or engaging in a sport you enjoy, you know what relaxation feels like, and you know when it's happening to you. I strongly encourage you to make relaxation a part of your daily life.

If you've felt robbed or shortchanged lately—if you've wondered, *Is this as good as it gets?*—remember that a life in Christ keeps getting better and better. Proverbs 4:18 says that "the path of the [uncompromisingly] just and righteous is like the light of dawn, that **shines more and more (brighter and clearer) until [it reaches its full strength and glory"** (emphasis added).

That means God has great things in store for your life! No matter how irritating, frustrating, or stressful the situation is that you're facing today, don't let it steal your hope or decrease your joy. If you'll trust God and learn to let go of the stress that is trying to hold you back, you'll be amazed at how much better life can be.

Things to Remember:

➤ Stress is a real enemy, capable of doing real physical, emotional, and spiritual damage. It's not something to be trivialized and swept under the rug.

➤ We don't have to live as victims of stress. As believers, we have been promised a new, powerful, overcoming life in Christ.

➤ Once you realize that stress is trying to keep you from experiencing God's best in your life, you can start making some necessary choices to change things.

➤ Five ways to de-stress: seek out social support; practice "shrug therapy"; find your comfort zone...and stay there; nutrition, proven supplements, healthy diet, and exercise; schedule time to relax.

Did you know?

Big stress or little stress—your body reacts the same way. The human body doesn't differentiate between a major or minor stress. Regardless of the catalyst, a typical stress reaction floods the body with a wave of 1,400 biochemical events. If this happens too frequently, we age prematurely, our cognitive function is affected, and we are drained of energy and clarity.[8]

KEEP
CALM
AND
CHOOSE TO
TRUST

CHAPTER 2

Who's in Charge?

When a train goes through a tunnel and it gets dark, you don't throw away the ticket and jump off. You sit still and trust the engineer.

—Corrie ten Boom

There are few things in life more stressful than thinking, *It's all up to me.*

It's up to me to make sure my children turn out great.
It's up to me to keep the house clean and tidy all the time.
It's up to me to figure out my future.
It's up to me to pay for my past mistakes.
It's up to me to provide all the things my children want.
It's up to me to change my spouse.
It's up to me to correct my coworkers.
It's up to me . . . It's up to me . . . It's up to me!

Whew! My stress levels started rising just writing those sentences. But that's how we live much of the time, isn't it? We assume that if something is going to get done, we have to be the ones in control. We say things like, "Just give it to me, and I'll do it!" or "I'll take it from here!" or "If I want something done right, I guess I have to do it myself!"

The problem with this mind-set is that it doesn't leave any room for God. The moment we begin to think *I'm in control* rather than trusting that *God is in control* is the moment stress has an opening in our lives. I understand there are times in life when we have to take decisive action. I'm not suggesting you sit back and do nothing. At work, with your family, around your friends—there are going to be plenty of opportunities for you to step up and boldly lead. We invite stress into our lives, not when we take right action, but when we try to take control.

God is good, and it is His desire that we place our trust completely in Him. He wants us to enter His rest, totally abandoning ourselves to His care. When we are able to believe and say, "God, I trust You," anxiety melts away. Psalm 37:3 says, "Trust (lean on, rely on, and be confident) in the Lord and do good." It's really that simple. When we make the daily decision to trust God's leadership while doing the good things we know to do, then He'll bring a harvest of blessings into our lives and meet our every need.

So let me ask you: Who has control of your life? Who do you trust to plan your future? Who do you rely on to set your course? Who do you depend on to provide what you need even when the need seems overwhelming? The answers to those questions go a long way in determining what kind of life you're going to live, overloaded or overcoming. Anytime we don't keep God first, life gets messy and we get stressed out.

> *Anytime we don't keep God first, life gets messy and we get stressed out.*

Road Trip!

A friend recently told me about a trip he took with his family. They traveled, by car, halfway across the country over a span of three days. The route he chose took them through mountainous regions, around bustling cities, and down long stretches of major highways. While he and his wife consulted their GPS, planned gas and meal stops, navigated through heavy traffic, and budgeted the travel expenses, he noticed his children were having the time of their lives in the backseat.

With each glance in his rearview mirror, he was struck by the kids' carefree attitude. They spent the trip watching movies on the computer, playing games on his wife's tablet, telling each other silly jokes, snacking from the fully stocked family cooler, enjoying travel games, and napping whenever they felt like it. When he saw how content and peaceful they were, he couldn't help but think, *Now* that's *the life!*

The picture of his children relaxing and enjoying the journey reminded my friend of how we can go through life as believers, content and carefree. He told me, "Joyce, my kids just trusted that I was in control. They knew I would get them to their destination safely. They didn't worry about how we'd pay for the trip, what the best route to take was, or how the car was running. I took care of all those things. Their job was simple: they just sat back, did what I asked them to do, and enjoyed the journey."

I think our lives would be much less stressful if we were more like those children. No wonder Jesus said we should have childlike faith (see Matthew 18:1–5). Those kids didn't try to take over the planning of the trip. They didn't ask to drive for a few miles. And they certainly didn't complain about the direction they were traveling. During the entire trip, they were content to let their father have control, because they trusted that he had a great plan.

This is how we can live out the journey of our lives. Rather than stress and worry about the direction we think we're headed in, rather than get upset when the road seems difficult, rather than wonder why it's taking so long—we can trust our Heavenly Father. We can let go of the steering wheel and turn it over to God, trusting that He has a great plan for our lives.

I have a strong personality, and I like to make decisions and work hard to accomplish my goals, but I understand that God is the one who sets the course for my life. It took me a long time to fully reach this place of peace, but thankfully, I've finally submitted my entire life to Him. So when a decision or an opportunity arises, I go to God first, asking Him if this is something He wants me to do. If I don't have peace about it, I don't do it. I can tell you, there have been numerous times I initially thought something was a good idea, but I didn't have peace about it when I prayed, so I let it go. And I was glad each time I did, because I discovered later that I would have been miserable had I accepted the task. The quickest way to peace is learning to submit every decision in your life to God. Stress has no say in your life when God is in control.

> *The quickest way to peace is learning to submit every decision in your life to God.*

I Can't Do It Without You

In Exodus 33, Moses is praying to God and he makes a rather direct (almost demanding) statement to the Lord. I suppose it was something he felt so strongly that he couldn't help but just blurt it out, hoping God would understand. Have you ever had a prayer like that? A prayer that was so desperate you didn't really take time to make it sound pretty, you just cried out to the Lord, trusting He would understand? (Hint: Sometimes those are the best kind of prayers.) If you have, you know how Moses felt, because that is exactly how he prayed.

This was a tough time for Moses and the children of Israel. In the previous chapter, the people had rebelled while Moses was meeting with God on Mount Sinai. Instead of waiting for Moses to return and tell them all the Lord had spoken, the people grew impatient and decided to fashion a golden calf to worship. The entire community, including Moses' brother, Aaron, had disobeyed God and suffered difficult consequences for worshipping at the altar of a false image.

So now, in chapter 33, God instructs Moses to pack up camp and continue the voyage to the Promised Land. God said in verse 1: "Depart, go up from here, you and the people whom you have brought from the land of Egypt, to the land which I swore to Abraham, Isaac, and Jacob." This sounds like good news, right? The journey was going to continue; God would once again be leading the children of Israel to their promised inheritance.

But there was a problem. God didn't intend to go

with Moses and the people. They would be traveling on their own. The Lord told Moses:

> *"Go up to a land flowing with milk and honey;* **but I will not go up among you**, *for you are a stiff-necked people, lest I destroy you on the way."*
>
> Exodus 33:3 (emphasis added)

At this moment, Moses had a decision to make. And this was a decision that carried high stakes. It would affect his future and the future of every person in the camp. Here were his options:

Option #1: Moses could trust in his own proven leadership ability and take over. He could charge forward, making the decisions and calling the shots. After all, Moses was born to be a leader. He knew how to make important decisions in the most crucial moments. This was his chance to be in charge!

Option #2: Moses could understand that if God wasn't leading them, neither he nor the children of Israel stood a chance. Why go anywhere if God wasn't going to go with them? Rather than moving, he could humbly, but boldly, ask God to forgive the people and take control of the journey.

Moses didn't hesitate in making his choice. In Exodus 33:15, Moses emphatically declares: "If Your Presence does not go with me, do not carry us up from here!" Did you notice the exclamation point at the end of that sentence? With all his energy, Moses basically said, *Lord, I'm not going* anywhere *without You!*

I love this bold statement by Israel's leader. Moses understood that he wasn't really the leader at all. Sure, God had given him responsibilities. And, yes, Moses had a part to play in the journey God had called the Israelites to take. But Moses understood that God was their leader—God was the one in control. And Moses knew that, without God, they would have no lasting success on their own. So Moses loudly proclaimed, "I'm not going anywhere without Your leadership, God."

The circumstances are different, but the options Moses faced are the same options you and I face today. When met with a dilemma or when pondering a decision, we can trust in our own ability to handle the situation, or we can trust God's leadership and ask Him to take control. And like Moses, the choice we make carries significant ramifications. If you go through life with the mind-set of "It's all up to me," you're going to live under the constant stress and worry that comes with dependence on self. But if you embrace a mind-set that understands "It's all up to God," you're going to be able to enjoy your life and go through each day stress-free.

So the question remains: Who is in control? Are you going to take *Option #1* and carry the weight of the world on your own shoulders, or are you going to follow Moses' example and choose *Option #2*, asking God to take control? The choice is up to you.

I remember when I was led by God to quit my job and spend time preparing for the teaching ministry God wanted me to pursue. We were going to be a little short each month of having enough money to pay our bills, and needless to say, I was very worried. I was so worried and afraid that at times my knees felt as if they would buckle underneath me and I would fall to the floor. On one particular day, I heard God whisper to my heart, "Joyce, you can try and do all of this by yourself, or you can trust Me to provide; it is up to you." I stopped right where I was and said, "I choose to trust You, Lord." I am happy to report that God was faithful and all the bills were always paid.

Quiz Time

Many people have been depending on themselves for so long (rather than depending on God) that they don't even realize they're doing it. Self-reliance can be the result of many different things. Some people begin depending on themselves as children because their parents are absent, dysfunctional, or abusive. Other people begin depending on themselves later in life when a spouse betrays them or leaves them. A lot of people just have such a strong personality that they've always tended to trust in their own abilities rather than looking to God first. And many others don't even know that trusting God with their lives is an option available to them.

Whatever the reason, I think we've established that your life will have so much more peace and happiness when you give God control. Proverbs 3:5 says it this way: "Lean on, trust in, and be confident in the Lord with all your heart and mind and **do not rely on your own insight or understanding**" (emphasis added). So, if you're not sure whether you're "leaning on the Lord" or "leaning on your own understanding," here is a little quiz that might help you figure it out:

The Control Quiz:

1. When faced with unexpected bad news, what is your first thought?
   a. How can I fix this?
   b. Oh, no. Here we go again!
   c. God isn't surprised by this news. He can work this out for good.

2. When talking about your future, are you more likely to begin a sentence by saying,
   a. "I don't have many options, but..."
   b. "If I work hard enough, I can..."
   c. "I know God has a great plan for me, so..."

3. When someone says something bad about you, are you more inclined to...
   a. return the favor
   b. ignore it (but remember how they hurt you)
   c. pray for that person, trusting God to defend you

4. If your kids are having trouble at school, do you...
   a. blame yourself for your parenting failures
   b. meet with the teacher
   c. ask God for wisdom and insight and *then* meet with the teacher

5. Which activity is more important for you each morning?
   a. Preparing yourself for the day
   b. Checking social media to see what others are saying
   c. Spending time with the Lord

This little "quiz" isn't meant to make you feel guilty if you discovered that you are not depending on God like you should. I just want to help you see how easy it is to fall into the trap of depending on self and thinking, *It's up to me!* That is such a stressful way to live—God has something so much better for you.

With God's help, we can move from dependence on self to dependence on God.

Several of the options listed above aren't necessarily bad or wrong, but they fall short of God's best. In each situation above, option "c" is an indicator that you're trusting God with control of your life. If options "a" or "b" best describe you, don't be discouraged. For many years, they described me, too. But with God's help, we can move from dependence on self to dependence on God. Simply start by asking God to show you each time you're trying to take over, rather than trusting Him. Normally, if I am trying to face a challenge in my own strength, I start to feel tense and that is an indicator to me that I need to ask for God's help.

I suggest you take a few moments each day to pray something like this: "Lord, I trust You with the direction of my life, and I give You control today. I'll do my part, and I'll work diligently as You guide me, but I won't receive the stress that comes from thinking I have to have all the answers. I know You have the answers, and I believe You will guide me to do what is right. I trust that You have a great plan for my life."

As we close this chapter, I want to share one last thing from Moses' story. After Moses prayed his bold prayer in verse 15, God answered him. God wasn't mad or offended by Moses' boldness. In fact, the opposite was true. God was pleased that Moses didn't want to go anywhere without His leadership. In Exodus 33:17, God responded to Moses by saying, "I will do this thing also that you have asked, for you have found favor, loving-kindness, and mercy in My sight and I know you personally and by name."

I want you to know that God feels the same way about you. God is not angry with you today. Like Moses, you, too, have "found favor, loving-kindness, and mercy" in God's sight, and He knows "you personally by name." So the next time you're faced with a stressful situation or a difficult decision, don't carry that burden by yourself. Go to God and ask Him to take control. He won't hesitate to answer you and show you the right path to take. You may need to be patient, but God is always faithful!

Things to Remember:

➤ There are few things in life more stressful than thinking, *It's all up to me!*

➤ God is good, and it is His desire that we place our trust completely in Him. He wants us to enter His rest, totally abandoning ourselves to His care.

➤ Every day we face two options: *I trust myself* or *I trust God.*

➤ Trusting God with your life doesn't mean you have no responsibilities or you don't make any decisions. It simply means that you submit each responsibility and decision to Him.

➤ You have found favor, loving-kindness, and mercy with God. He knows you personally by name!

Did you know?

Oil of anise, basil, bay, chamomile, eucalyptus, lavender, peppermint, rose, and thyme are all soothing scents that can help decrease stress levels.[1]

KEEP
CALM
AND
BE CONFIDENT

CHAPTER 3

The Best Stress-Relief Possible

Sorrow looks back. Worry looks around. Faith looks up.

—Ralph Waldo Emerson

In preparation for this book, I knew it was important to write not only about the causes but also about the cures for stress. If we don't understand the cures for stress, knowing the causes isn't very helpful—it's just discouraging. In this chapter I want to talk about a foundational cure that is highly effective because it is a preventative measure. This can stop stress in your life before it ever gets a foothold.

The quickest way to beat any problem is to be aware the problem exists, know the answer, and implement the solution *before* the problem gets out of hand. If you can prevent the crisis before it begins, life is much easier and more enjoyable. Have you noticed this to be true?

Let me give you some examples:

- It's easier—and more effective—to teach good behaviors to young children than having to correct wrong behaviors when they're older.
- It's easier—and more effective—to maintain a healthy weight with proper diet and exercise than going on a crash diet the week before you need to fit into that special outfit.
- It's easier—and more effective—to be alert in class and study a little each day than it is to stay up all night cramming for tomorrow's exam.

In other words, if you know the solution ahead of time, you can *act* wisely rather than *react* hurriedly. This is a key to victory in every area of your life… and that includes overcoming stress. In this chapter, I want to help you understand the answer ahead of time so you never again have to react to a stressful situation with a feeling of panic and fear.

But first, let's look a little more closely at what stress is and how it affects your body. Stress in its most basic form is a type of panic. It is a jolt to our nervous system that results from a perceived danger.

> *Stress in its most basic form is a type of panic. It is a jolt to our nervous system that results from a perceived danger.*

Every stressful situation we face brought on by our mind or emotions has the same effect on our bodies as a real crisis situation.

I've read several descriptions of what happens to the body when it reacts to a stressful situation. The stressor, whatever it may be, causes an impulse to be sent to the brain. The brain combines emotions with reasoning. With this process, the person reacting to the stressor analyzes the situation. If he perceives it as threatening, his body engages the "fight or flight" response.

The nervous system responds in three ways. First, it directly stimulates certain body systems—the heart, muscles, and respiratory system—with electrical impulses to cause a quick increase in heart rate, blood pressure, muscle tension, and respiration.

Secondly, it signals the adrenal medulla, a part of the adrenal gland, to release the hormones adrenaline and noradrenaline, which alert and prepare the body to take action. This reaction begins a half-minute after the first, but lasts ten times as long.

And third, the nervous system stimulates the hypothalamus in the brain to release a chemical that stimulates the pituitary gland. The pituitary gland releases a hormone that causes the adrenal glands to continue releasing adrenaline and noradrenaline and to begin releasing cortisol and corticosterone, which affect metabolism, including the increase of glucose production. This third, prolonged reaction helps maintain the energy needed to respond in a threatening situation. Nearly every system of the body is involved, some more intently than others, in the response to the stressor.

Every time we become excited, stimulated, or upset, even though we may not realize it, our entire system is gearing up for either fight or flight to defend itself from the perceived threatening or dangerous situation.[1]

Then when we calm back down, our body comes out of that emergency state and begins functioning normally, in the way it is supposed to function most of the time. The next time we face a stressful situation or become upset, the whole process starts over. And so it goes, up and down according to our changing mental and emotional states. This is what our bodies go through when we face a perceived crisis. As you can imagine, the effects of excessive stressing and unstressing can have long-lasting and far-reaching consequences.

So stress, in its most basic form, is a reaction—it's a panic. It is your body's way of saying, "Something bad has happened; I have to fight or flee." In times of real danger, this physical and emotional reaction can be a benefit, but most of the things we stress about aren't real dangers—they're perceived dangers. *What if I lose*

Most of the things we stress about aren't real dangers—they're perceived dangers.

my job? I wonder if they like me? How am I going to get all this done? These anxieties and hundreds of others just like them trigger your "fight or flight" reflex in an unhealthy, harmful way.

Now that you know what stress is doing to your body, let's look at how to stop it dead in its tracks before it can start this damaging cycle.

Preventative Medicine

Confidence is an essential key to preventing stress. When you live with confidence, stress has little to no effect on you. But I'm not talking about self-confidence. Self-confidence may be helpful to have, but even the most self-confident person should know his or her limitations. The kind of confidence I am talking about is confidence in God. It insulates us from the damaging effects of stress. God wants us to have confidence (faith and trust) that He is working on our behalf.

In the last chapter, we talked about the decision to give God control of your life. That is so important, because now that you know God is in control, you no longer have to worry about the pressures and anxieties others worry about. You can be confident even in the face of the most stressful situations.

Imagine if you were playing a neighborhood

basketball game and the best player in the NBA was the captain of your team. Would you be worried about the outcome? Of course not! You would have the confidence to challenge all takers. Or what if you were singing a duet at the local talent show and you just happened to have the world's most famous vocalist as your friend and duet partner. Would you freak out before you went onstage? Of course not! You would sing with confidence, knowing that her talent would carry you both through. This is how it is with God. When you have a confident assurance that God is on your side—that He is working on your behalf—you can shrug off the things that used to make you cower in fear.

This is exactly what King Jehoshaphat learned to do. The Bible tells us his story in 2 Chronicles 20. At the beginning of the chapter we see that three armies had joined together to attack Jehoshaphat and the people of Judah. The Bible says it was "a great multitude" of soldiers that were coming against them. As you can imagine, this was a very stressful situation. Though Jehoshaphat was initially afraid, he didn't panic. Instead, the king went to God in prayer because he knew God was in control. The odds were certainly against Jehoshaphat and his army, but when God is on your side, the odds don't matter. God responded to Jehoshaphat by saying:

You shall not need to fight in this battle; take your positions, stand still, and see the deliverance of the Lord [Who is] with you, O Judah and Jerusalem. Fear not nor be dismayed. Tomorrow go out against them, for the Lord is with you.
2 Chronicles 20:17 (emphasis added)

Before the battle began, before a single sword was drawn or arrow was shot, God assured Judah and King Jehoshaphat that the battle would be won... because God was fighting for them! He was doing the work on their behalf.

This is the same thing that God is saying to you today. There is no need to worry about or be afraid of any perceived lack, struggle, or uncertainty that you may face; God is on your side! He is going to provide everything you need. He is going to fight the battle for you. All you have to do is "take your position, stand still, and see the deliverance of the Lord [Who is] with you."

It's Already Taken Care Of

Have you ever had someone come up to you and say, "I need to tell you about a problem, but before I tell you, I want you to know you don't have to worry; I've already taken care of it"? As the leader of a worldwide ministry organization, I've had this happen quite a few times—I was informed about a problem but assured it had been taken care of and there was nothing I needed to worry about.

This is the kind of confidence we can have with God. There are going to be stressful events and situations in our daily lives, but we can have an internal assurance that God has already taken care of it. He has already gone before us and prepared the way that we might walk in it (Ephesians 2:10). We might not see the solution right away, we might not know exactly how God is going to fix the problem, but we can be assured that He will...because that is the promise He gives us in His Word. Our part is to trust God and His part is to provide the answer we need!

> *Our part is to trust God and His part is to provide the answer we need!*

Here are just a few of God's promises to build your confidence:

- ***It is the Lord Who goes before you***; *He will [march] with you;* ***He will not fail you or let you go or forsake you***; *[let there be no cowardice or flinching, but] fear not, neither become broken [in spirit—depressed, dismayed, and unnerved with alarm].* (Deuteronomy 31:8; emphasis added)

- *Fear not [there is nothing to fear], for I am with you…**yes, I will help you; yes, I will hold you up** and retain you with My [victorious] right hand of rightness and justice.* (Isaiah 41:10; emphasis added)
- *And my **God will liberally supply (fill to the full) your every need** according to His riches in glory in Christ Jesus.* (Philippians 4:19; emphasis added)

These promises (and many others throughout the Word of God) are the key to stopping stress before it ever begins. When a problem arises, before hitting the panic button and initiating the physical and emotional roller coaster of stress, remember that God has promised that He is going before you and He is going to make a way for you—even when there seems to be no way (Isaiah 43:19). Confidence that God is always working in your life is preventative medicine. If you have this confidence, you have implemented a solution before you even get the problem of stress.

Let's look at this practically:

Let's say Bill receives a call from his doctor's office saying they'd like him to come back in and have some additional tests next Friday. Bill has a choice to make. He can spend the next week in a panic, miserable and afraid, wondering what might be wrong, or Bill can defeat stress before it even begins. He can say, "Lord, I'm not going to assume the worst. I know You are working on my behalf. I thank You for my health, and with Your help, I'm going to choose peace over stress this week." That doesn't mean that Bill never feels concerned or anxious; it just means he's confident that God is working on his behalf and that no matter what the outcome of the tests are, God is in control.

Or what about Sally...

Sally has a major decision to make. Now that the kids are old enough to go to school, she's debating between reentering the workforce and staying at home. Both choices have pros and cons, but she just doesn't know which decision to make, and she is starting to lose sleep over it. In this situation, stress is already creeping in. Sally is losing her joy because she is afraid she'll make the wrong decision. This is a perfect opportunity for Sally to regain her confidence in the Lord. If Sally will remember that God is in control and He is working on her behalf and on the behalf of her family, she'll make her decision without fear. Rather than being afraid she'll make the "wrong choice," she'll know God will provide no matter what—He has *already taken care of it*. Now Sally can relax and confidently go with the decision that brings her the most peace. She can step out in faith and trust that if her decision is right, God will open all the right doors that need to be opened.

Let's talk about Jennifer . . .

Jennifer recently enrolled in a continuing education program at her local community college in order to get the high school diploma she never earned as a teenager. It took a lot of courage for Jennifer to go back to school ten years later, but now she is second-guessing herself. She's starting to worry about spending the money for the classes and wondering if she's even capable of passing. Jennifer has a choice to make. She can worry or she can stand in confidence, knowing that God will provide everything she needs. This is a chance for Jennifer to defeat stress before it even begins. She can pray, "God, I know I can do all things in Your strength, and I know that if I have the right attitude, this is going to be a great experience." If Jennifer will trust that God has *already taken care of it*, she'll move forward confidently and meet her goals.

Instead of reacting in a panic, wondering how you are ever going to make it through, you can choose to act in confidence.

Okay, I've mentioned Bill, Sally, and Jennifer, but what about you? What situation are you facing in life that is causing you to ride the roller coaster of stress? Whatever it is, I want to encourage you to change your thinking. Instead of *reacting* in a panic, wondering how you are ever going to make it through, you can choose to *act* in confidence. God fought the battle for King Jehoshaphat when the odds were against him, and God can do the same for you. Stand confidently, knowing that God has already taken care of it— whatever *it* may be. He is working on your behalf, and when He is on your side, there is no way you can lose. Remember: worrying is completely useless. It never provides any good benefits at all, but when you place your faith in God, it opens a door for Him to work!

The Confidence to Jump

In his book *Holy Sweat*, author Tim Hansel tells a story about hiking with his young son. While climbing some cliffs out in the country, Hansel heard a voice from above yell, "Hey, Dad! Catch me!" He turned around just in time to see his son, Zac, flying through the air, already having sprung from a rock high above.

Hansel dove to catch his son and they both went tumbling to the ground. Zac loved it! Exasperated, Hansel gasped, "Zac! Can you give me one good reason why you did that?" His young son replied with a quiet confidence, "Sure. Because you're my dad."[2] It was that simple. Young Zac knew that his father was there to catch him.

I've met a lot of people who haven't jumped in a long time. Rather than leap in confidence, springing toward the opportunities and challenges of life, they're sitting still, frozen in fear. Worry, anxiety, and stress have been like anchors holding them down. With white knuckles and quivering voices, these people spend their days saying things like, "It might not work," "What if I fail?" and "I'm just so nervous."

But this doesn't have to be you. You can be a person who defeats stress and has the experience of enjoying an exciting and adventurous life. It doesn't matter how high the ledge or how treacherous the trail, you can take that leap for one reason— your Father is there to catch you. He's been with you the whole time, and He has been working on your behalf. Don't be worried or afraid. If God leads you to do something, jump with confidence and live a life that defeats stress before it even gets started.

Things to Remember:

➤ Though we may not realize it, stress causes our entire system to gear up for either fight or flight to defend itself from a perceived danger.

➤ A confidence that God is working in your life will keep you from panicking when faced with a stressful situation.

➤ When God is on your side, there is no way you can lose.

➤ The best way to defeat stress is refusing to push the panic button—confidence that God is with you will give you the strength to stay calm and at peace.

➤ Whatever the "it" is...God has *already taken care of it!*

Did you know?

The stress hormone cortisol causes abdominal fat to accumulate, and it enlarges individual fat cells, resulting in what researchers call "diseased" fat.[3]

KEEP
CALM
AND
MAKE
A CHANGE

CHAPTER 4

I'd Like to Exchange This

It is not how much we have, but how much we enjoy, that makes happiness.
—Charles Spurgeon

Linda stumbled through the door just before sunset, exhausted from a busy day at work. Groceries in one arm, purse and computer in the other, she exhaled in relief, glad her workday was finally over. Her two boys, David and Aaron, stopped playing their video game long enough to say, "Hi, Mom. What's for dinner?" and her husband, Will, came in from mowing the lawn just in time to ask the same question. It looked like it would still be a little while before Linda could relax.

But dinner would have to wait. There was one bright spot in Linda's busy day that she wanted to show Will and the boys first. On her lunch break, Linda had gone down to her favorite store and bought a beautiful blouse for an upcoming night out with friends. It was a top she had been wanting for months, and today's big sale afforded her the opportunity to buy it. Even on sale, it wasn't cheap, but it was so beautiful, Linda just couldn't pass it up.

Excitedly, Linda tried on the blouse and came out to show her hungry family. Will exclaimed, "Wow! Looks great, hon!" and the boys glanced up from their video game to say in unison, "Nice shirt, Mom." But when Linda spun around to let Will see the back, things took a negative turn.

Apologetically, Will informed his wife, "Um, honey, I don't know how to tell you this, but there is a big rip in the back of your blouse." Linda ran to the bathroom to look in the mirror, and sure enough, her new blouse had a tear in the back. She couldn't help it. The events of the stressful day finally overwhelmed her, and Linda burst into tears. Nothing had gone right all day and her beautiful, new, *ripped* blouse was the proverbial icing on the cake.

Will came in to the bathroom and gave his sobbing wife a huge, comforting hug. "Don't worry, honey," he said. "You can take it back tomorrow and exchange it for a new one." That's when Linda replied in a way that surprised her husband. As she wiped her eyes and worked to compose herself, she said, "No. I don't want to go through all that hassle. I'll just make do with it the way it is. Maybe I can wear a jacket over it and no one will notice that it's ripped."

Bewildered, Will stepped back and said, "Linda, that's silly. You don't have to go around wearing a torn blouse. That doesn't make any sense. Let's just take it to the store and exchange it for a new one." But Linda persisted. "No. It'll be fine. I'll just wear it the way it is. If no one sees my back, they'll never know the blouse is ripped. I'm not going to exchange it. I'm going to hold on to it and deal with it."

Three nights later, Linda sadly wore her ripped blouse as she went out with her friends for dinner. It was a night she had looked forward to for weeks, but she really couldn't enjoy herself. Rather than talking and laughing and having a good time, she spent the evening feeling uncomfortable because she knew she had a huge rip in the back of her blouse. Everyone else had a wonderful time, enjoying the dinner and making the most of their girls' night out, but Linda never got in on the fun. Instead, she spent the evening self-conscious, frustrated, and unhappy.

It would have all been different if she had made one simple decision: I'm going to make the exchange.

It could have been easily avoided. Linda could have been just as happy as her friends that night. She didn't have to spend the evening uncomfortably hot because she couldn't take her jacket off. She didn't have to be upset and unhappy. In fact, she could have been the happiest person in the room, wearing a beautiful new blouse and relishing much-needed time with wonderful friends. It would have all been different if she had made one simple decision: *I'm going to make the exchange.*

It's Really Not That Complicated

If reading that fictitious story about Linda frustrated you, you're not the only one. You were probably thinking (like I was), *C'mon, Linda. Just return the blouse. It's not complicated—make the exchange.* It's an unfortunate reality that Linda had a problem, but she also had a solution. All she had to do was take advantage of the solution and exchange the blouse for a new one. (Don't worry, things get better for Linda by the end of this chapter.)

You know, stress is kind of like that ripped blouse. Stress is something that happens in our lives—and many times—through no fault of our own. Linda didn't cause the rip; it just happened. We don't always cause stressful situations; they just happen. Whether you're fifteen, fifty-five, or eighty-five, you're going to deal with stress on a regular basis. And you know what? It's not easy. Whether it's a demanding boss, a bigger-than-expected bill, an upcoming move, an avalanche of homework, a disappointing diagnosis, a calendar that is too full, or an unruly child, stress from these and other situations

> *Stress is something that happens in our lives—and many times—through no fault of our own.*

can be enough to make you run to the bathroom and have a good cry.

But the good news is that as believers, we don't have to take ownership of the stress. We don't have to hold on to it and incorporate it into our daily lives. In other words, we don't have to go to a dinner party with a ripped blouse. We can exchange that stress for something better. The Word of God teaches us that we can cast our cares on God (see 1 Peter 5:7) and exchange the burdens, frustrations, and sorrows of the world for the joy of the Lord.

Just look at these Scriptures that talk about the exchange that happens for the children of God:

> *Be not grieved and depressed, for the joy of the Lord is your strength and stronghold.*
>
> Nehemiah 8:10

> *To give them beauty for ashes, the oil of joy for mourning, the garment of praise for the spirit of heaviness.*
>
> Isaiah 61:3 (NKJV)

> *Weeping may endure for a night, but joy comes in the morning.*
>
> Psalm 30:5

It's really not that complicated—God wants to make a trade with you. Of course, the ultimate trade is the exchange of your sins for Christ's righteousness (see 2 Corinthians 5:21), but that is just the first in many wonderful exchanges. God wants you to give Him all your cares, problems, and failures. In return, He'll give you His peace and joy. And on top of that, God promises that He is the one who is going to protect and take care of you.

In order to exchange your stress for His peace, it is important that you stop getting upset about little things that you can't control. Many people would like for God to take care of them, but they insist on worrying or trying to figure out an answer on their own, instead of waiting for God's direction. Many of us wonder why God doesn't give us peace, but the truth is that He has already given it to us, with an instruction to stop allowing ourselves to be agitated and disturbed (see John 14:27).

> *In order to exchange your stress for His peace, it is important that you stop getting upset about little things that you can't control.*

What a great trade! We give God our stress, and His peace is ours! We give Him all our cares and concerns, and He gives us His protection, stability, and joy. That's the privilege of being cared for by Him. Because He cares for us, He wants us to live in joy. God wants you to make the exchange each and every day because He loves you and He has a wonderful plan for your life.

Which Are You?

At the beginning of this chapter, you and I were both a little frustrated with Linda. Why in the world would she choose to go around with a ruined blouse? Why wouldn't she just make an exchange? Well, I want to take a moment to make this a little more personal. Is it possible that you're more like Linda than you realize? Maybe you're not going around with a ruined blouse, but are you letting the stresses and pressures of the world destroy your peace, steal your joy, or ruin your happiness? I meet people all the time who are living far short of what God has for them, but they don't even realize it. They've held on to stress for so long, they can't see how it has damaged their lives. I don't want that to be you, so let me share three questions for you to ask yourself and some specific ways to make an exchange for God's best today. Take a moment and consider this. Are you:

1. *Stressed or at rest?*
   It seems that there are so many people overwhelmed, stressed out, exhausted, and weary because of the demands of life. But the truth is we don't have to live that way. In Christ, it's possible to live in God's rest and find relief from the demands of stress and worry.

In Christ, it's possible to live in God's rest and find relief from the demands of stress and worry.

The truth is we all get weary. There's absolutely nobody who doesn't get overburdened at times. If you think it's just your life that you get weary about, I can assure you that it wouldn't be any better if you had somebody else's life. It's not life that makes us tired; it's the way we handle life. Our attitudes and mind-sets cause us to be stressed more than our circumstances do.

In Matthew 11:28–29, Jesus said, "Come to Me, all you who labor and are heavy-laden and overburdened, and I will cause you to rest. [I will ease and relieve and refresh your souls.] Take My yoke upon you and learn of Me, for I am gentle…and humble…and you will find rest (relief and ease and refreshment and recreation and blessed quiet) for your souls." The rest Jesus is talking about in this passage of Scripture is not a rest from doing any work—Jesus is talking about an inner rest for your mind, will, and emotions. This is a rest you can have in the midst of even the most hectic situations!

In order to be at rest rather than overloaded and stressed, the first step is simply to come to God. This is something you can do on a daily basis. Rather than facing the day in your own strength, you can come to Him each morning and say, "Lord, I'm depending on you today. Help me to have joy and peace regardless of the situations around me." The next thing to do is to take His yoke upon you. This means that whatever task is before you, ask God to help you and give you His strength. Then together, you and God can handle anything that comes along.

Let's make this practical:

- ☐ If you're tired and weary because of an ongoing struggle with a coworker, make an exchange today. Simply pray and say, "Lord, I'm exchanging my stress for Your rest. I give this situation to You and ask You to work all things together for my good."

- ☐ If you're tired and weary because of a child who keeps trying your patience, make an exchange today. Rather than getting angry and losing your temper, ask God to give you wisdom. Trade in your frustration for His direction and trust that a divine breakthrough is going to take place.

- ☐ If you're tired and weary because you've spent so much energy trying to change your spouse (and it's not working), make an exchange today. Rather than asking

God to change your spouse, ask God to change *you*. You'll be surprised at what a difference it will make!

Whatever the situation is that has you stressed out, choose to trust God and be at rest on the inside. When the pressure rises and tempers start to flare, ask God for an inner peace that passes understanding so you can live a life that is calm, stable, and at rest.

2. *A worrier or a grateful worshipper?*

Worry and worship are exact opposites. We'd all be happier if we spent more time worshipping God, thanking Him for our blessings, and less time worrying about our problems. Worry opens the door for stress, but living with an attitude of worship brings us into God's presence. One key to living a joy-filled life is to take our eyes off the circumstances around us and fix them on the Lord.

Sometimes, when we are going through something difficult, stress and frustration work to keep us from worshipping God. It's easy to get so preoccupied with our problems that we forget the promises of God. But when we know that God has our best interests

> It's easy to get so preoccupied with our problems that we forget the promises of God.

at heart, we can worship Him regardless of our circumstances. Remember, God is good even when our circumstances are not. You can worship God regardless of any situation you are going through, because God has promised to never leave you or forsake you (see Deuteronomy 31:6). You don't have to give in to worry or despair; you can worship God, knowing that He is going to carry you through.

So stop worrying about everything. Give it to God and worship Him every day. Let Him know that you love Him and that you appreciate all the things He does for you. Don't waste another day of your life worrying. Determine what is your responsibility and what is not. Don't try to take on God's responsibility. When you do what you can do, God steps in and does what you can't. So give yourself and your worries to God and begin enjoying the abundant life He has planned for you.

Let's make this practical:

□ If you're worried about something that is going on in your family, make an exchange. Rather than rehashing the same old problem, take a few minutes to worship and thank God for His goodness. Remember some of the problems He has solved for you in the past, and trust that He will do it again.

☐ If you're worried about what you heard someone is saying about you, make an exchange. Instead of worrying and calling everyone you can think of to defend yourself, worship God for being your defender (see Psalm 59:9). Praise Him that He is strong enough and caring enough to protect you against the accusation of others.

☐ If you're worried about losing your job or not getting that promotion, make an exchange. Don't focus on what might go wrong; instead worship God for what is going to go right. Take a few minutes to celebrate that He is your provider (see Philippians 4:19) and He is going to supply everything you need for today and each day to come.

Don't let worry ruin your life. If you'll take time each day to focus on God and His love and goodness, your life will be characterized by worship. Worshippers aren't stressed and frustrated. Worshippers are full of joy because they know their God is powerful and that He is able to fulfill His promises in their lives.

3. *Hectic or happy?*
Lily Tomlin once said, "For fast-acting relief, try slowing down."[1] I like that quote because there

are so many people who have stuffed their cal-
endars with so many things to do that they are
stressed and burned out by life. An important
factor in enjoying a peaceful, joy-filled life is
learning to be obedient to the Lord. Following
the Holy Spirit will always lead you into peace.
He will never lead you into stress, because He is
the Prince of Peace. Common sense tells us that
God's not going to stress us out and lead us to
do more than we can do; however, we often do
this ourselves.

It's so important not to overcommit ourselves. Do you have too much to do? This
seems to be one of the biggest complaints I hear
today. People say, "There's just too much to do
and not enough time to do it all." (Sound familiar?) I've found that this is often the result of
not saying no often enough. Sometimes we say
yes and commit ourselves to do something that
we really don't want or need to be doing. We
take it on just to keep other people happy. We
really need to be careful in this area and make
sure that our mouths are not saying yes when
our hearts are say-
ing no.

So let me ask you
a few more questions
regarding "happy or

*Whose pace are you
moving at? Are you keeping
the pace God has set for
you or someone else's?*

hectic." Whose pace are you moving at? Are you keeping the pace God has set for you or someone else's? Are you stressed out from trying to keep up with everyone else? Living under the stress of competition and comparison? A perfectionist with unrealistic goals?

I believe you can be happy in the middle of a hectic world, but it'll require some decisions—possibly radical ones—on your part. Allow God's Spirit to lead you out of a stressful lifestyle and into one of peace and joy. Respect your body. Treat good health and feeling good as a valuable gift. Don't waste the energy God has given you trying to do too many things. Use your energy to enjoy the important things God has placed in your life and learn to let some of the other things go.

Let's make this practical:

☐ If you're hurried and overloaded by too many daily commitments, make an exchange. Look at your calendar and ask God to show you what things you need to step back from. It might not be easy, but decide to only give your energy to those things that bring you peace rather than take it away.

☐ If you're hurried and overloaded by a morning routine that is hectic and rushed, make an exchange. Decide to prioritize in order to make your mornings more productive. Rather than staying up late the night before, go to bed earlier. Instead of oversleeping, get up a few minutes early and spend time with the Lord. You'll be amazed at what a difference a more disciplined routine makes.

☐ If you're hurried and overloaded because you're comparing yourself to someone else and trying to do all the things they are doing, make an exchange. Instead of living their life, determine to live your own. Ask God to help you reject the temptation to compare yourself to someone else and decide to be content and happy with who He has made you to be.

It's amazing how something as practical as your daily schedule and routine can raise or lower the stress levels in your life. Don't let the pressures and anxieties of life make you run all over the place, never taking a moment to enjoy the life God has given you. Instead, determine to live at God's pace and to relax and savor every day He has given you.

Back to Linda and Her Ripped Blouse

Let's finish the chapter by going back to unhappy Linda. Even though she's fictional, I feel we need to resolve her story because she represents so many of us—needing to make an exchange but reluctant to do so. Let's take a moment and rewrite the story so that Linda can have a blast with her friends for their girls' night out.

You remember the setting, right? Linda has come home from a stressful day. Her boys, David and Aaron, are playing video games but thinking about dinner. Her husband, Will, has just come in from mowing the grass. And even though she's exhausted, Linda is excited to show her family the new top she bought during her lunch hour, because she wants to wear it in a few days for a fun dinner party with friends…

Excitedly, Linda tried on the blouse and came out to show her hungry family. Will exclaimed, "Wow! Looks great, hon!" and the boys glanced up from their video game to say in unison, "Nice shirt, Mom." But when Linda spun around to let Will see the back, things took a negative turn.

Apologetically, Will informed his wife, "Um, honey, I don't know how to tell you this, but there is a big rip in the back of your blouse." Linda ran to the bathroom to look in the mirror, and sure enough, her new blouse had a tear in the back. She couldn't help it. The events of the stressful day finally overwhelmed her, and Linda burst into tears. Nothing had gone right all day and her beautiful, new, ripped blouse was the proverbial icing on the cake.

Will came in to the bathroom and gave his sobbing

wife a huge, comforting hug. "Don't worry, honey," he said. "You can take it back tomorrow and exchange it for a new one"...

As she wiped her eyes and worked to compose herself, she said, "You're right, Will. I'm just a little disappointed and overwhelmed by the events of the day. But tomorrow I'm going to exchange this blouse and get a new one, because I really like it."

The next afternoon on her lunch break, Linda returned the ripped top to the department store where she bought it. The sales associate apologized profusely and quickly exchanged the blouse for another just like it, but in perfect condition. Even though Linda had gotten the blouse on sale, the sales associate took an additional 15 percent off in an effort to show good will. Linda showed it off again that night for Will and the boys, and they loved the way it looked on her.

Three nights later, Linda happily wore her new blouse as she went out with her friends for dinner. They all commented on how lovely she looked, and she had a wonderful time laughing and talking over dinner. She even told the story of the ripped blouse, hungry boys, understanding husband, and convenient exchange. It was a great night out with friends and a beautiful ending to the story all because Linda made one simple decision—a decision that you and I can make each and every day—she decided to make the exchange!

Things to Remember:

➤ We don't always cause stressful situations. Sometimes they just happen.

➤ You don't have to hold on to stress. You can exchange it for the peace and joy of the Lord.

➤ God wants to give you beauty for ashes, the oil of joy for mourning, the garment of praise for the spirit of heaviness (see Isaiah 61:3 NKJV).

➤ No matter how stressful situations on the outside appear, you can have an inner peace and rest.

➤ If you're filled with worry, worship is the key. You can't be a worshipper and a worrier at the same time.

➤ Don't let your schedule control you. Instead, take control of your schedule and ask God to give you the wisdom to do only the things that He has called you to do.

KEEP
CALM
AND
DO YOUR PART

SIMPLE WAYS TO DE-STRESS:

- ✓ Go for a walk
- ✓ Put your phone away
- ✓ Watch a funny movie
- ✓ Cut back on the caffeine
- ✓ Write down your worries…then throw them away
- ✓ Spend time with a close friend
- ✓ Enjoy a new hobby
- ✓ Get some exercise
- ✓ Plan ahead so you're not so rushed
- ✓ Perform a random act of kindness
- ✓ Read a good book

CHAPTER 5

Decisions You Make and Steps You Take

Peace is a journey of a thousand miles and it must be taken one step at a time.
—Lyndon B. Johnson

When you woke up this morning, you probably made some decisions. You decided how many times to hit the snooze button. You decided what outfit you were going to wear. You decided how many cups of coffee to have. But there were some other decisions you didn't get to make (even though I bet you wish you could have). Let me show you what I mean...

> When you woke up this morning, did you get to choose what the weather would be like today?
> Did you decide how light or heavy traffic would be on your way to work or when you were driving around town running errands?
> Did you have a say in what news headlines would flash across your television set or fill your Twitter feed?

How about the mood of your spouse or your coworkers? Did you get to choose what kind of mood they would be in when they met you for lunch?

I guess those are kind of silly questions. Neither you nor I get to make those types of decisions. If we did, the temperature might be a few degrees warmer, the traffic would certainly be much lighter, the news would be filled with positive, feel-good stories, and our spouses and friends would always be in fantastic moods. Sounds wonderful, doesn't it?

We may not be able to choose what happens in the environment around us, but we can certainly choose how we respond to it.

The truth is we don't get to make any of those external decisions, but that doesn't mean we're victims of our circumstances. We may not be able to choose what happens in the environment around us, but we can certainly choose how we respond to it. And the decisions we make on a daily basis go a long way in determining the kind of life we are going to live. You can make decisions and you can take steps to change how you view your circumstances and how you respond to them.

Think of it like this:

- If it's raining outside, you can take care of the inside chores you need to do but have been putting off.
- If traffic is heavy on your normal route, you can choose an alternate route to save time.
- When the news is negative and depressing, you can look for other media outlets that report better stories.
- If your friend is in a terrible mood, you can lift her spirits by encouraging her rather than letting her mood affect you.

These are some simple examples that illustrate a greater point: Even though you can't control every situation you face, you can control how you face it. You can take steps to determine what kind of life you are going to live. Ralph Waldo Emerson said it this way: "Nothing external to you has any power over you."[1]

> Even though you can't control every situation you face, you can control how you face it.

So many people who are overloaded by stress, pressure, and anxiety in life feel like victims. They wrongly assume everything is everyone else's fault and there is very little, if anything, they can do about it. *Their jobs are too stressful. Their friends are unsympathetic. Their kids are too demanding. Their pasts are hard to get over. Their spouses are uncaring.* The list goes on and on. But do you see the common theme? Burdened, overloaded, stressed-out people are focused on the circumstances around them rather than the steps in front of them.

I want to encourage you today. If you feel burdened and troubled in life, with God's help, you can take a step to change your outlook and overcome your situation. You are not a victim. No matter what you've been through, you don't have to give in to the pain of the past or the pressures of the present. You can decide to take steps in order to live a new life in Christ filled with peace and joy.

Do What You Can Do and God Will Do What You Cannot Do

We began this book by talking about the importance of trusting God in order to keep ourselves from being overloaded in life. We looked at how vital it is to let God have control and I encouraged you to remember that God is working tirelessly on your behalf. It is a great comfort to know that God will always do His part. But guess what? You have a part to play, too! Isn't that exciting? We all have an assignment from God and He always gives us the grace (undeserved favor and power) that we need to do our part.

Trusting God, and waiting on Him, is not a

passive activity. There are always steps you can take...even when you're waiting on God. Specifically, there are always steps you can take to overcome stress. (I'll give you some specific steps in a moment.) If you do what you can do, then God will do what you cannot. Do your part to reject every worry and anxiety and God will come through in ways that will amaze you.

I study diligently for my sermons, and when I stand up to present the material, quite often I hear myself saying things I did not even know that I knew. What happened? I did my part and God came through supernaturally with some things to make the message even better. Had I been lazy or passive and thought I didn't need to prepare, those supernatural things would not have happened.

So many people don't take *any* steps because they don't know *all* the steps, but you don't have to have it all figured out to take an action step. Rather, you get to decide to be active or inactive. You don't have to worry about the part you don't know how to do— just do the part you know. Your faith-filled actions are seeds you sow. Sow your seed in faith and God will bring a harvest at just the right time.

You don't have to be prepared to do the entire job by yourself; just prepare yourself to do the best that you can do and remember that God will add what you don't have. So let me say it one more time: If you will do what you can do, then God will do what you cannot. For example, if you need a job, you can go look for one. That is something that you can do, and if you do it, then God will help you get the right job. You cannot make a company hire you, but God can change the heart of the king (those in charge) even as He changes the course of the water flowing in rivers (Proverbs 21:1). God will give you favor!

A little boy gave his lunch and Jesus added His power to it and fed thousands of people (see John 6:9–13). The boy didn't have enough to feed the crowd, but he did what he could and Jesus did the rest.

Every Step Is Important But…

The Bible is a book full of action. There are many stories of God acting miraculously on behalf of His people, and there are many promises of His divine intervention in our lives; however, there are also many stories of regular people just like you and me taking steps (physically and spiritually) in order to pursue God's best in their lives.

To give you examples, I will remind you about the children of Israel who marched around the city of Jericho once a day for six days—and seven times on the seventh day (see Joshua 6). These obedient followers of Joshua took a lot of "steps" before God gave them a great and miraculous victory.

Or consider the woman in Luke, chapter 8, who had been sick and bleeding for twelve years. You may remember her story. Even though she was considered "unclean" by the religious laws of her day, she didn't let that keep her from taking action. This woman moved through the crowd, pushing past every person who stood between herself and Jesus. She "stepped" right up to the Lord in order to touch the hem of His garment to receive a miracle.

And consider the men in Capernaum who carried their paralyzed friend to see Jesus (see Mark 2). These men had incredible faith and determination. Even though the house where the Lord was teaching was filled to capacity, they refused to give up. These dedicated friends climbed the "steps" to the roof and lowered their friend down into the house in order for Jesus to heal him. That is some serious determination and a great example of taking action steps.

Every step you take is important, but perhaps the most important step is the first one.

I want to look at another story that I think will help you get started today in your pursuit to overcome stress. You see, every step you take is important, but perhaps the most important step is the first one. Because if you can take the first step, it gives you confidence to know you can take a second step... and then a third... and then a fourth... and so on.

Before you know it, you'll be going farther with God than you ever thought possible.

Matthew, chapter 14, tells us the familiar story about Jesus' disciples being caught in a terrible storm. Verses 24–25 show us how they spent the night fighting for their lives on the Sea of Galilee as the unrelenting storm raged all around them. (Talk about a stressful situation!) But even though the disciples thought they were alone, they weren't. The Bible tells us that in the fourth watch of the night (between 3:00 a.m. and 6:00 a.m.) Jesus came walking to them on the water. Of course, the disciples were terrified. Not only had they been fighting this storm all night, but now they thought they were seeing a ghost. (The stress just keeps building!)

While the other disciples are panicking, Peter says something amazing in verse 28. He cried out to Jesus, "Lord, if it is You, command me to come to You on the water." Of course, you know the story. Jesus responds to Peter by simply saying, "Come!" In other words, Jesus said, "I'll do My part, but I want you to do your part, too. You get to choose. Are you going to sit in fear or are you going act in faith? Come on out!" And that's when it happened…

Peter took a step!

Can you imagine how difficult that first step must have been? From the boat to the water? From the known to the unknown? Peter was stepping out in faith, regardless of the circumstances around him. I imagine he had doubts. There may have been a part of him that thought, *This is absolutely crazy!* But Peter chose not to live stuck in passivity. He took a bold first step.

> Even though Peter's faith faltered, it was still greater than any of the other disciples who never got out of the boat.

Of course, Peter's stroll on the water with Jesus was short-lived. He walked with Jesus on the water at first, but eventually, the wind and the waves distracted him and he took his eyes off the Lord. As he began to sink, he cried out for help, and Jesus rescued him before calming the storm. But even though Peter's faith faltered, it was still greater than any of the other disciples who never got out of the boat, and it teaches us a great lesson today—even when our faith fails, Jesus still rescues us. If we take the steps He asks us to take, He will always help us reach our destination.

Maybe as you're reading this today, you feel like you're dealing with a storm in your life. Maybe you know what it's like to be afraid and unsure of how things are going to work out. And maybe you understand how easy it is to do nothing because you're afraid of where that first step might take you.

If that's the case, I want to remind you that as long as you focus on the storm rather than on God's promises for your life, you're always going to be frustrated, afraid, and stressed out. But God has a better life in store for you. And if you want to live His abundant, confident, joy-filled life, it's time to understand that you have a part to play. You can't sit back in fear and passivity; instead, you can act in faith and take that bold first step. You may not be sure how it's going to work out. You might not know what the next step is going to be. But if you do your part, there is one thing you can know for sure: God promises He will do His part in your life.

It Might Look Like This

Every process has a beginning, a middle, and an end. And each of these parts is important. If you are going to really enjoy the life Jesus died to give you, you'll need to learn the importance of starting well (beginning), being consistent (middle), and finishing what you've started (end). None of us is perfect, and we all make mistakes from time to time, but the more we study the Word and the closer we get to God, the more we'll learn to be balanced in each of these areas.

For the purposes of this chapter, I want to give you some practical ways to have a great beginning and take a big first step against stress today. No matter how intimidating the circumstance or how hectic your life may seem, you can do your part today to reject an overloaded life and receive God's promises for you and for your family. Here are a few ways to do that...

Your First Steps to Defeating Stress:

1. If your finances are a source of constant stress in your life, decide to start a budget (or reevaluate your current budget). What is something practical you can do to solve the problem? Cut an expense that is a luxury. Look for a new way to make some additional money. Ask someone who is good with finances to look at your budget and give you some suggestions.

2. If there is someone who is driving up your stress levels by constantly hurting your feelings, do something nice for them—send them a kind note, buy them lunch, tell them something you appreciate about them, or begin praying for them on a regular basis. By doing these little things, you are taking steps of faith and obeying God's command to love your enemies.

3. If a nagging health problem is leaving you feeling stressed out and run down, start an exercise routine. No more excuses.

Exercise takes energy, but it gives you back more energy than it takes!

Set aside time each day to get the exercise and care your body desperately needs. Rather than making excuses, make a plan...and stick to it. You may think that you simply don't have the energy to exercise. You feel too bad, or you're too tired. But I often find when I go ahead and begin to exercise, I start to feel better. Exercise takes energy, but it gives you back more energy than it takes!

4. If the demands of work are overwhelming and causing you to feel overloaded, do something about it. Delegate some tasks, reevaluate your systems, or talk to your boss. (Your boss may not even realize how much you are doing or how it is negatively affecting your personal life.) Instead of complaining how overworked you are, look for ways to be more efficient and how to make the most of your time each day.

5. If you're disappointed your church hasn't recognized your gifts and what you have to offer, start volunteering in a ministry that interests you. They may not even know what you are passionate about or gifted to do. Rather than sitting back and waiting for someone to approach you, take a step and start serving with a great attitude.

6. If you have a big project to do and it is causing anxiety because you don't know where to

begin, make a plan. Write down some small daily goals that will eventually add up to a big success...and then meet those goals each day. Don't try to do it all at once. Do a little bit each day until your ultimate goal is met.

7. If you constantly feel "under the gun" or under stress and you can't pinpoint the exact reason, start making some biblical daily confessions. Rather than getting up each day, talking about how bad things are, begin each day declaring God's Word and His promises over your life. "I am more than a conqueror!" (Romans 8:37) "God will provide for my every need!" (Matthew 6:26–33) "I can do all things through Christ who strengthens me!" (Philippians 4:13)

These are just a few examples, but as you can see, there are so many ways you can step out in faith in order to live the life Jesus died to give you. God is going to do His part, but He wants you to do your part, too. You may not have all the answers and you may not get it right every time, but if you'll determine to take a step, God is going to meet you along the way. Remember, you don't have to live a life burdened with stress and frustration. Instead, you can live a happy, peaceful, overcoming life. It's just a matter of what steps you are going to take. The choice is yours...you get to decide.

Things to Remember:

➤ You don't get to choose what happens around you, but you do get to choose how you respond to it.

➤ The decisions you make and the steps you take each day determine what kind of life you are going to live.

➤ If you'll do what you can do, God will do what you cannot.

➤ When you take a step for God, even if your faith fails, God won't let you sink.

➤ No matter how intimidating the circumstance or how hectic your life may seem, you can do your part today to reject an overloaded life and receive God's promises for you and for your family.

Did you know?

Stress can make acne worse. Researchers say stress-related inflammation rather than a rise in sebum (the oily substance) is to blame.[2]

KEEP
CALM
AND
REMEMBER
GOD'S GOODNESS

CHAPTER 6

Did You Forget Something?

It's not the situation, but whether we react negative or respond positive to the situation that is important.

—Zig Ziglar

Can I tell you something about myself that not everyone knows? I'm not particularly good with noises. The truth is, certain noises can really stress me out! If there is an annoying squeak in the car or if my refrigerator rattles when the motor comes on, it really annoys me. My first reaction is, *We need to get that fixed…now!* Do you know what I mean? Are you like that, too? For some reason, I just get easily annoyed and frustrated by obnoxious, repetitive noises.

Well, as you can imagine, this makes things interesting when I'm on the road. I travel a lot, preaching the Word nationally and internationally, and it seems that every new hotel has some new noise to test my patience. Sometimes it's a thumping air conditioner, other times it's a dripping faucet or a running toilet, and a lot of times it's other guests talking loudly in the hallway in the middle of the night. I've gotten better at dealing with it, but these things tend to really bother me.

I remember one time in particular that was especially bad. The hotel where we were staying had an incredibly loud truck that would pull up right outside my window first thing each morning. I don't know what kind of truck it was—a garbage truck or maybe a delivery truck—but when it backed up, it made that loud *BEEP, BEEP, BEEP, BEEP* sound. Normally, this would be enough to push me over the edge. It was so loud! How in the world was I supposed to get any rest?

But something different happened on this particular trip. In the middle of the obnoxious *BEEP, BEEP, BEEP, BEEP* that woke me up, I heard another sound. It was much quieter, but I could make it out very clearly—birds were singing. The truck didn't bother them; they were chirping away. I remember thinking, *I'm going to focus on the beauty of those birds singing rather than that truck beeping.*

It sounds like a little thing, I know, but I just decided to shift my focus from what was bothersome to what was beautiful. And you know what? It changed my entire outlook on the situation. I didn't get frustrated. I didn't lose my temper and think, *Can't someone make that truck leave? Why do these things always happen to me?!?* Instead, I had a different mind-set. I thought, *If those birds can have joy in the middle of all the noise, I guess I can, too!*

Of course, the singing birds didn't drown out the noise of the truck. I could still hear the distracting clamor outside my window. But now I had a completely different outlook, because my focus had shifted. Rather than obsessing on the loud and the loathsome around me, I chose to hear the lovely instead. And it made all the difference in the world. It wasn't too long before the truck left, and I felt I had a huge victory because with God's help, I didn't get frustrated.

The Cure Many People Overlook

I tell you that story because what you focus on will often determine your stress level. One of the biggest causes of stress is focusing on the negative things that are happening around us and allowing those things to fill our hearts with frustration, fear, or anxiety.

Many people get so consumed with what is going wrong they can't see anything else—their full attention is given solely to their problem. Other people they know experience challenges also, but they are convinced their problems are more difficult than anyone else's. They are consumed with their own problems and make them the priority in their lives. If the sink backs up, their day is ruined. If the car starts to idle funny, they go into a panic. If their child gets a poor grade at school, they question every parenting decision they've ever made. Do you see what's happening? They're focusing on the negative, and that focus is filling them with frustration and despair.

There is rarely a day that goes by that is without some kind of challenge. If I focus on everything that is wrong, I can ruin my day. I spent many years of my life focusing on the wrong things. I was rarely happy in those days; it was like I was expecting something to go wrong just so I would have an excuse to get mad. Looking back on it, it amazes me how I used to lose my joy over some of the dumbest things. If someone was rude to me in line, if Dave stayed too late at the golf course, if a restaurant messed up my order—even the smallest "problems" or inconveniences of life would send my stress levels soaring.

Thankfully, the Lord began to teach me how to set my attention on the good things in my life. I began to realize that the more time I spent obsessing about the things I was unhappy about, the more power I gave to those things. With God's help, I began to see that I didn't have to let daily problems or inconveniences determine my happiness (or lack of happiness) any longer. When I began to take time each day to focus on God's goodness and His blessings in my life, my perspective changed, my attitude improved, and my joy increased like never before! Just this morning I wrote down several things in my journal that I am thankful for. I find that if I purpose to look for good things and make a big deal out of them, it keeps me from focusing on the negative things.

It's really pretty simple: If focusing on what is going wrong is a *cause* of stress, naturally a *cure* for stress is to focus on what is right. When we look at the positive things that God has placed in our lives, it gives us a sense of perspective, stability, thankfulness, and balance. And all four of those things (perspective, stability, thankfulness, and balance) are remedies for stress. It is wise and healthy to hold on to the good things in your life and let the negative, stressful things fall by the wayside.

> *If focusing on what is going wrong is a cause of stress, naturally a cure for stress is to focus on what is right.*

The Word of God has much to say when it comes to focusing on the positive rather than the negative. Here are a few verses that remind us that we can choose to set our sights on God's best. The author of Hebrews wrote:

> **Fixing our eyes on Jesus**, *the pioneer and perfecter of faith.*
> Hebrews 12:2 (NIV; emphasis added)

In his letter to the church in Colossae, the apostle Paul wrote:

> And **set your minds and keep them set on what is above (the higher things)**, *not on the things that are on the earth.*
>
> Colossians 3:2 (emphasis added)

And I especially love what Paul said in the book of Philippians:

> *Whatever is true, whatever is worthy of reverence and is honorable and seemly, whatever is just, whatever is pure, whatever is lovely and lovable, whatever is kind and winsome and gracious, if there is any virtue and excellence, if there is anything worthy of praise,* **think on and weigh and take account of these things [fix your minds on them].**
>
> Philippians 4:8 (emphasis added)

Notice that Paul doesn't say we should just *occasionally* think about the good things—he says we are to "fix our minds on them." That means each and every day, we should take the opportunity to think about what we are thinking about. Rather than dwell on all that is going

Rather than dwell on all that is going wrong, we can choose to dwell on all that is going right!

wrong, we can choose to dwell on all that is going right!

What you think about—what you focus on—is going to affect how you see life. If you'll determine to focus on God's goodness and His promises that are true, pure, lovely, kind, and gracious, you won't succumb to the bullying behavior and tactics of stress. When others are frustrated, discouraged, and fed up with their lives, you'll have a totally different attitude. No matter what happens during the course of your day, you'll be able to trust God and respond differently than you used to. You won't be panicked; you'll be peaceful! You won't be overloaded; you'll be overjoyed! That's what happens when you choose to focus on the good things God *has* done and *is* doing on your behalf. You will also be able to encourage those who are focused on negatives. When God gives us His grace to enjoy our lives in the midst of difficulty, it is important to let Him use us to pray for and help those who are still in bondage.

Things to Remember

Have you ever forgotten something? (I know I have.) Maybe forgotten where you put your car keys? (Yep, I've done that.) What about someone's birthday? Have you ever forgotten to buy a birthday gift for a friend or loved one? (Guilty. I've done that, too.) Someone recently told me that her mom once left her at a grocery store because she forgot she had brought her along. Her poor mother got halfway home before making a panicked and speedy U-turn to retrieve her fuming teenage daughter. (Thankfully, I've never done that.)

I guess we've all forgotten things. And we've all dealt with the fact that forgetting things can have consequences. One consequence is stress! If you forget where you put your car keys, you're going to be stuck at home and feel the stress of it. If you forget someone's birthday, you run the risk of hurting his or her feelings and it will probably add stress to your life. And if you forget your teenage daughter at the local grocery store…well, she may make sure you feel stressed over it, and you'll probably have to take her shopping to make up for it.

But there are other things we forget that have even bigger consequences—life-altering consequences. This is true for many Christians today. There are so many Christians who are forgetting something extremely important. And this forgetfulness is causing their level of stress to increase and their level of joy to decrease. Let me show you what I'm talking about. In Psalm 103: 1–2, look at what David said:

> Bless (affectionately, gratefully praise) the Lord, O my soul; and all that is [deepest] within me, bless His holy name! Bless (affectionately, gratefully praise) the Lord, O my soul, and **forget not [one of] all His benefits** (emphasis added).

Did you see that? What a powerful instruction for you and me today: "Forget not [one of] all His benefits." There are a lot of things we may forget over the course of a day, but the benefits and blessings of God shouldn't be on that list. The goodness of God is something we can choose to place at the forefront of our minds. There are two things I want to point out about this verse:

1. You have benefits as a child of God!
    That's something to get excited about! The dictionary defines *benefit* as "a favor conferred; advantage; profit."[1] That's what you have been given! And David doesn't say you have only one benefit; he uses the plural *benefits*. That means you have been given many "favors" and "advantages" as a child of God.

    The benefits aren't something we've earned by impressing God. They are things He freely gives us because we are His children and He loves to bless us. This is why Romans 8:17 says, "And if we are [His] children, then we are [His] heirs also: heirs of God and fellow heirs with Christ [sharing His inheritance with

    > The benefits aren't something we've earned by impressing God. They are things He freely gives us because we are His children and He loves to bless us.

Him]." You've inherited the benefits, the blessings, and the goodness of God!

2. It takes a conscious effort to remember God's goodness.

The reason David gave this instruction to remember God's goodness is because it's easy to forget. You wouldn't think so, but it happens all the time. We can get so caught up in the busyness of life, and we can get so distracted by the difficulties we face, that we simply forget all the good things God has given us.

It's interesting to point out that David was actually talking to himself when he wrote this verse. He begins by saying, "Bless...the Lord, O *my* soul." David knew how easy it was to forget what God had done, and he understood that slipping into a negative mind-set was a dangerous trap. That's why he reminded himself to focus on God's blessings. And if it was important to David, it should be important to us. You and I can do the same thing today.

Your List of Benefits

One of the things I love about the Bible is how practical it is for daily living. Not only does Psalm 103 encourage us to remember the benefits we have as children of God, but it also goes on to give us a list, showing us what many of those benefits are. Take a look at some of the benefits from Psalm 103 and, like David, encourage yourself to "affectionately, gratefully praise" God for His goodness in your life!

- Your sins are forgiven!
  "Who forgives [every one of] all your iniquities." (v. 3)
- Healing is yours!
  "Who heals [each one of] all your diseases." (v. 3)
- God has redeemed your life! (You have a new life in Him.)
  "Who redeems your life from the pit and corruption." (v. 4)
- You've been made beautiful, dignified, and noble!
  "Who beautifies, dignifies, and crowns you." (v. 4)
- God loves you unconditionally!
  "With loving-kindness and tender mercy." (v. 4)
- You've been cared for and provided for!
  "Who satisfies your mouth…with good." (v. 5)
- You're strong, overcoming, and soaring!
  "Your youth, renewed, is like the eagle's [strong, overcoming, soaring]!" (v. 5)
- God is your defender!

"The Lord executes righteousness and justice [not for me only, but] for all who are oppressed." (v. 6)

- God is not mad at you!
"The Lord is merciful and gracious, slow to anger and plenteous in mercy and loving-kindness." (v. 8)
- When you mess up, God will forgive you!
"He has not dealt with us after our sins nor rewarded us according to our iniquities." (v. 10)
- God knows you better than you know yourself!
"For He knows our frame." (v. 14)
- No matter what happens, God will never stop loving you.
"But the mercy and loving-kindness of the Lord are from everlasting to everlasting." (v. 17)

And this is just the list from one chapter! The Bible is full of many more blessings and promises of God for your life. So the next time you feel your peace slipping away and your stress picking up steam, take a moment to stop and remember the benefits you've been given as a child of God.

The next time you feel your peace slipping away and your stress picking up steam, take a moment to stop and remember the benefits you've been given as a child of God.

What Do You Hear?

I don't know what you're going through today that has brought a level of stress into your life. Maybe you're dealing with something big like the loss of a loved one, a marriage on the rocks, a personal betrayal, or a significant health scare. Or maybe you're dealing with an issue (or multiple issues) much smaller in scale. Sometimes it's the little things like a deadline at work, a gossiping neighbor, a broken washing machine, or a missed opportunity that stress us out the most.

Whatever it is you are facing, let me encourage you to tune out the loud sound of the truck and listen for the lovely song of the birds. I know the negative things in your life can cause quite a commotion, but if you'll listen carefully, you'll hear a much more beautiful refrain. God's goodness, His favor, His blessings and provision are all around you. If you set your heart and your mind on the positive things He has done for you, you'll be surprised at how quickly your peace and joy will return.

David gave us a lengthy list of wonderful spiritual benefits to contemplate in Psalm 103, but there are simpler things, too. Gifts and talents you have been given, family members who love you, clothes on your back, a roof over your head, a job that pays the bills, friends who stand by your side. When times get tough and your stress levels start to rise, take a moment to think about both the simple and the profound blessings of God in your life. If you'll remember God's goodness, you'll forget to be stressed... and that's one thing you'll never regret forgetting!

Things to Remember:

➤ One of the biggest causes of stress is focusing on the negative things that are happening around us.

➤ What you think about—what you focus on— is going to affect how you see life.

➤ If focusing on what is going wrong is a *cause* of stress, a *cure* for stress is focusing on what is right.

➤ When we look at the positive things that God has placed in our lives, it gives us a sense of perspective, stability, thankfulness, and balance.

➤ Psalm 103 instructs us to "forget not" God's benefits and then gives us an entire list of benefits that are ours as children of God.

Did you know?

Stress makes the blood "stickier" in preparation for an injury. Such a reaction, however, also increases the probability of developing a blood clot.[2]

KEEP
CALM
AND
SIMPLIFY
YOUR LIFE

CHAPTER 7

Choice Overload

Trop de choix tue le choix.
(Too much choice kills the choice.)
—French proverb

Too much of a good thing…can actually be a bad thing. I know that sounds strange, but it's true. Here, let me show you. Just as an exercise, why don't you take a moment and think about a few things that are "good" or fun in your life. Now, consider that those things, if taken to an extreme, can actually be harmful. I'll prove it to you:

Craig is a college student, and he loves sleep. He sleeps past noon most days, and the second he gets back to his dorm room after class, he collapses onto his bed for a lengthy nap. There's nothing wrong with sleep, is there? Sleep is a good thing; we all need it. But if Craig sleeps all the time, he'll be late for class, neglect homework assignments, and feel lethargic.

Jenny loves sweets. In fact, she craves them. There is nothing she appreciates more than a good dessert. And while sweets are a delicious snack—something we all enjoy from time to time—if Jenny never uses discipline and goes overboard on eating sugary foods, she is going to deal with serious health and body image problems.

Sherri loves her job. It's challenging and a great source of income for her family. She never complains when big projects land on her desk, and she doesn't hesitate to work late into the night and even on weekends if need be. Now, there is nothing wrong with work. Working hard to provide for your family is a good thing. But if Sherri allows herself to overdo it at work—never resting, never coming home, neglecting her family— she can burn herself out and grow distant from those she loves most.

We could go on and on. Spending some time at the beach is a good thing—too much time on the beach will damage your skin. Money is a good and necessary thing—too much money has ruined the lives of many people. Wanting to be your best is a good thing—driving yourself to perfectionism can be harmful to you and to all those around you.

I'm sure there are exceptions, but that doesn't change the truth that if we experience too much of a good thing, it can actually turn out to be a bad thing in the long run. I've seen it time and time again: excess of any kind can be very dangerous. This is why the Word of God says, "Let your moderation be known unto all men." (Philippians 4:5, KJV). Moderation is important. There is wisdom in getting past *I don't have enough of something* but stopping short of *I've got way too much of something.* Balance is key!

This same principle that is true for sleep, food, work, money, ambition, and so on (all good things in moderation) is also true for the "choices" you and I have in life. I think we would both agree that having choices is a good thing, but I've noticed that having *too many* choices can negatively affect us and actually bring us a tremendous amount of unnecessary stress. In her *New York Times* article "Too Many Choices: A Problem That Can Paralyze," Alina Tugend notes that the more psychologists and economists study choice overload, the more they are coming to the conclusion that "an overload of

Having too many choices can negatively affect us and actually bring us a tremendous amount of unnecessary stress.

options may actually paralyze people or push them into decisions that are against their own best interest."[1] Too many choices can bring confusion, uncertainty, and elevated levels of stress.

There is no denying that we have more options than ever before in current culture. We have hundreds of television channels to choose from, coffee options galore (like grande, chai, venti, decaf, iced, frappe, spiced, just to name a few), and an incredible variety of handheld electronic devices that let us tweet, text, follow, favorite, snap, watch, and listen. Every time we turn around, we're bombarded with new things to try, new plans to sign up for, and new choices to make.

I read recently that the average American supermarket now carries 48,750 items (more than five times the number in 1975).[2] Now *that's* a lot of items to choose from! No wonder a missionary friend of mine had a hard time buying cereal when he and his wife visited the States. It wasn't that they couldn't find any cereal. They found the cereal aisle just fine. But they were so overloaded by the number of options, they walked out empty-handed, shaking their heads in dismay. You see, in Africa, where they lived, they had one choice of cereal, so it was not stressful at all to choose.

Whether it's how we spend our money, how we

spend our energy, or how we spend our time, if we allow ourselves to get distracted by the diz-zying array of modern options, we can easily

If we allow ourselves to get distracted by the dizzying array of modern options, we can easily fall into the stress trap.

fall into the stress trap—what should be a good thing turns into an exasperating thing. People fall into this trap all the time. Buying a new house becomes a bur-den, picking a phone plan takes months, finding a church turns into a competition, and starting a new diet is something people seem to do every other week. In his book *The Paradox of Choice*, Barry Schwartz correctly notes that it is at this point that "choice no longer liberates, but debilitates."[3]

Making a Choice When Life Gets Crazy

If you've ever felt stressed out and overloaded in the face of multiple options, I have good news for you: You can be a person who makes wise, bold, confident decisions. You don't have to go through life indeci-sive and unsure. And you don't have to be intimi-dated any longer by the sheer number of choices before you. With God's help, you can cut through the distractions and make strong decisions that will build your peace, not your stress.

Here are five steps to staying calm and making great choices when facing countless options:

Step #1: Ask God for Direction

Hebrews 13:6 says, "So we take comfort and are encouraged and confidently and boldly say, 'The Lord is my Helper; I will not be seized with alarm [I will not fear or dread or be terrified].'" The fact that God is a help to us should fill us with great calm and confidence. Anytime there is a decision to be made, we can go to God and ask for His guidance and direction. After all, the Word promises that He will help us!

> *Anytime there is a decision to be made, we can go to God and ask for His guidance and direction.*

I've noticed that so many people wait and go to God as a last resort. *After* they have tried everything they can think of, or *after* they have made a decision that didn't work out, *then* they go to God in a panic and beg for help. But that is a backward process. That's like going out and buying a coat the last day of winter. You need a coat before the cold arrives, not after.

In the same way, we need God's direction before we make a decision, not after. Rather than going to God as a last resort (which is a very stressful way to live), make it a practice to go to Him first thing. I finally learned to do this on a regular basis, and I encourage you to do it, too. No matter how big or how small the decision you are facing, ask God for His wisdom. Ask Him to show you what to do and when to do it…and then believe He is leading you as you go forward. If you'll make a determination to always talk to God about the choices you are facing, you'll notice a new level of contentment in your life.

Step #2: Simplify the Decision-Making Process

Henry David Thoreau said, "Our life is frittered away by detail…simplify, simplify."[4] Simplicity is so important to enjoying life. The fact is we contribute to a lot of the stress we face by making things very complicated and complex. Sometimes we view upcoming decisions like we're playing a chess match. We're thinking three steps ahead and making it a lot more complicated than it needs to be. In the midst of choice overload, it is crucial that you simplify your decision-making process. There are different ways to do this, but here are three suggestions to simplify things:

1. Be content with where God has you.
   Contentment is a key to simplicity. The apostle Paul said, "For I have learned how to be content (satisfied to the point where I am not disturbed or disquieted) in whatever state I am"

(Philippians 4:11). Paul had known trouble and triumph, poverty and prosperity—and he had learned to be content regardless of his situation. Contentment isn't about external circumstances; contentment is about an inner peace. If you'll settle down, trust God, and enjoy where He has you at this moment, decision-making will become much easier.

2. Slow down.

For so many people, the pace of life is way too fast. They're running from event to event, activity to activity, without ever slowing down to enjoy life. Much of this activity is fueled by a fear that they will miss out on something. And anything that is fueled by fear is unhealthy and spiritually dangerous. They may also feel pressured to do everything that everyone wants and expects them to do. They are stressed out simply because they don't know how to say no.

Good decisions are rarely made in a rush.

Good decisions are rarely made in a rush. If you find that you're having a hard time finding peace in the midst of all the daily decisions you need to make, I encourage you to slow down. Don't panic—take time to enjoy your life and lean on God to help you make your decisions.

Jesus was always busy, but He was never rushed. He wasn't running around, stressing out at the thought of all the things that had to be done. Look to Jesus as your example today. Don't let the accelerated rush of life cause you to leave peace behind.

3. Reduce your options.

If you're facing a decision or a dilemma that has many, many possible answers, this is a simple way to decrease the stress potential. You may not know the exact right answer, but I bet you can determine which answers are wrong. Rather than get upset by the complexity of the choice, just start eliminating any and every bad option. You might be surprised by how helpful this exercise is. Sometimes, the more you whittle away the bad options, the more obvious and apparent the right option becomes.

Here are three simple examples: If you need to buy cereal and you're confused by the choices, eliminate all the ones that have a high sugar content and your choice options will be greatly decreased. Starting your day with a bowl full of sugar is not a good, healthy choice. You eliminate the bad option and it is easier to find the right one.

I was wearing a top yesterday that is new and I really like it. It is pink and that is a color that

I rarely find in a style I like. However, all day I had to pull the top down because the material was slippery and it kept sliding up around my waist instead of covering my hips. It began to frustrate me and I felt I had to check on where it was every few minutes. The simple choice is not to wear it again! Even though I really like it, I don't want the stress it will add when I wear it. I can simplify my day by eliminating the option that will frustrate me.

I find that my stress level goes up when I try to make things work for me that simply are not working. Have you ever kept trying to wear a pair of shoes that hurt your feet and leave blisters every time you wear them? I have, but I have decided that choosing an option that is comfortable is less stressful than being uncomfortable just because my shoes are cute.

Step #3: Seek Good Advice

Independence is a good trait, but like anything else, if it is out of balance, it can be a disadvantage. I think it's wonderful to be strong and not live your life dependent on what others say, but there are times when the opinions of others can be very beneficial. Don't mistake pride for independence. Sometimes, the best thing you can do is humble yourself and ask a friend for help.

When dealing with a choice overload, it may be wise to ask a trusted friend or counselor for advice. Proverbs 11:14 says, "Where no wise guidance is, the people fall, but in the multitude of counselors there is safety." So it is often very helpful to get help from people you trust. Many times there are people around you who have already gone through what you're facing, and their opinions can be invaluable.

However, it's important that you don't feel like you have to do what someone else says just to make them happy. Balance is important here. Let God lead you, not the opinion of others. Be wise enough to seek truly helpful counsel at strategic times and then bring that advice to God and ask Him to give you peace about the decision He wants you to make.

My daughter had literally thousands of decorating choices to make when she and her husband were building their home. Since decorating is not a strong gift for her, she felt stressed by all the choices. It was much easier for her to have others help her select perhaps two or three options and then she picked from those. However, my daughter-in-law is great at decorating and she won't need any help at all. It is wise to know yourself and never be too independent to ask for the help you need.

Step #4: Be Confident and Decisive

The problem with too many choices is that it saps us of our confidence. Even if we feel like we've made a good decision, we wonder if we've made the absolute best decision. It's like ordering at a restaurant that has a fourteen-page menu. When there is an over-abundance of options, it takes longer to order. Doubt creeps in, asking you, "Are you sure that's what you really want?"

Indecision may not be a big deal at a restaurant, but it can be crippling in life. In order to simplify the decision-making process, it is important that we move forward with confidence and decisiveness. A person without confidence is like a car sitting in a driveway with no gas in the tank. The car has the ability to travel, but if it doesn't have any gas, it's not going anywhere. Confidence is our fuel. Confidence will carry you forward—past doubt, around indecision, and over uncertainty.

Confidence will carry you forward—past doubt, around indecision, and over uncertainty.

Rather than thinking, *What if I get this decision wrong?* choose to have confidence that you will get it right. Remember, you've already asked God for His wisdom and guidance. He is with you, and He is going to help you. And you know what? If you make the wrong decision, God sees your heart and He knows you are trying to do what is right. He's going to be there to get you going back in the right direction. So don't make decisions out of fear any longer—move forward in confidence!

Step #5: Let Peace Make the Call

Even after asking God for help, simplifying the decision-making process, getting good advice, and moving forward with confidence, there are still times when we can't help but wonder, *Am I really making the right choice?* And when the stakes are high and a lot is on the line, this can be a stressful question. If you're considering a new job, whether or not to move across the country, which school to enroll your children in, if you should get married, and so on—you probably want to make sure you get it right the first time. People ask me all the time, "Joyce, how do I really know which decision to make?"

When people ask me this (and maybe you're asking it now), I always tell them what the apostle Paul said in Colossians 3:15. This is a great verse to remember when you are in the final stages of making an important decision: "And let the peace (soul harmony which comes) from Christ rule (act as umpire continually) in your hearts [deciding and settling with finality all questions that arise in your minds, in that peaceful state]." In other words...let peace make the call!

Which of your options do you have the most peace about? After you've prayed about it, sought wise counsel, discarded the bad options, and confidently considered the best remaining options, what gives you the most peace? That feeling of peace is often a confirmation that it is God's best. Trust that He is pointing you in that direction and let peace settle "with finality all questions that arise in your mind."

I also recommend that with any important decision, even after you feel that you have peace, it is good to let your decision sit in your heart for a period of time. This helps me because if I feel the same way for two or three weeks, I am even more assured that I am making the right decision.

You Have a Guide

An overload of choices can be a very stressful thing if you are expected to make those choices on your own, but thankfully you're not. It is so comforting to know that God has promised to be with you. No matter how big or small the decision you are facing,

No matter how big or small the decision you are facing, you can be at peace, knowing that you are not expected to make that decision on your own.

you can be at peace, knowing that you are not expected to make that decision on your own. Not only is God with you, but He is also going to give you the guidance you need to look past the numerous options and make a wise choice. John 16:13 says that the Holy Spirit "will guide you into all the Truth (the whole, full Truth)." The fact that the Holy Spirit is your guide makes all the difference.

Imagine if you were expected to travel down the Amazon River with no guide. Wow…talk about stress! You'd probably be worried all the way down the river. You wouldn't be able to enjoy a single second of the journey because you'd be thinking about all the things that could go wrong. Snakes, alligators, rainstorms, spiders the size of your hand—there's no way you'd have any peace. You'd be overloaded with stress for sure.

But it would be a completely different story if an experienced guide were leading you down the river. If you knew your guide would keep you safe and help you every step of the way, you'd be much more relaxed. Anytime you were unsure what to do, your guide would protect you, teach you, comfort you, and inspire you to keep going. You'd learn new things and enjoy new experiences in an exotic location—it could be the trip of a lifetime!

You may be thinking, *Joyce, there's no way I'm going down the Amazon River!* But I used that example for a reason. Choice overload is kind of like a jungle. Too many choices and you can get intimidated and overwhelmed, thinking about all the things that could go wrong and all the dangerous repercussions you might face. But let me remind you today that you are not traveling alone. The Holy Spirit is your guide and He promises to give you wisdom and lead you into all truth. So don't be stressed out by the choices you face today. Ask God to help you see past the distraction of choice overload, trust His guidance, and get ready because He wants to take you on the trip of a lifetime.

Things to Remember:

➢ Too much of a good thing can actually be a bad thing.

➢ Having options is good, but having too many options is a common source of stress.

➢ When faced with a decision, going to God is a first option, not a last resort.

➢ You can simplify the decision-making process by being content, slowing down, and reducing your options.

➢ It is wise to seek good advice from trusted friends or leaders, but don't feel you have to do what they say just to make them happy.

➢ What is the choice you have the most peace about? If you're not sure which choice to make, let peace make the call.

➢ The Holy Spirit is your guide. If you ask, He will give you the wisdom you need. You're not left alone to make this decision on your own.

Did you know?

Laughing lowers stress hormones (like cortisol, epinephrine, and adrenaline) and strengthens the immune system by releasing health-enhancing hormones.[5]

KEEP
CALM
AND
LAUGH

CHAPTER 8

Laugh, Laugh, and Laugh Some More

A good laugh is sunshine in the house.
—William Thackeray

Picture it for a moment: You're on an isolated beach, enjoying a beautiful day. The wind is in your hair. The water is the absolute perfect temperature. Your phone isn't ringing, the boss isn't e-mailing you about a stressful project that is overdue, and there are no demands weighing on your mind. You've already made dinner reservations at a local restaurant that has great reviews, and the only thing you have to do between now and dinner is…relax.

Ah, vacation. Sounds pretty great, doesn't it? Whether it's the beach, the mountains, a camping trip, or just a week off to stay at home and unwind, vacations are a great way to relax, refresh, and recharge. It's a time to leave the worries of work and the stresses of daily life behind and just enjoy fun, carefree days with family and friends.

But recent studies show that many people don't

take advantage of their vacation days—particularly here in America. Concerned that they'll fall behind at work or that someone else might take their job, American workers use only half their eligible paid vacation time. And when they do take vacations, 61 percent work while they are supposed to be relaxing, despite complaints from family members.[1] Study after study reveals that vacation days are an unused benefit.

I tell you that because I believe laughter is a lot like an ignored vacation day—it's an unused benefit. Unfortunately, laughter is an opportunity that many people neglect to take full advantage of. It's available to all of us—we could enjoy it if we chose to—but it remains in a queue of benefits that is often overlooked. Rather than seeking out opportunities to laugh and enjoying even the smallest things in life, many people go through each day frowning and frustrated—discouragement crowds out delight; problems overshadow playfulness.

It may seem like a little thing, but laughter is vitally important in the battle against stress, anxiety, fear, and worry.

God has given us the ability to laugh for a reason. It may seem like a little thing, but laughter is vitally important in the battle against stress, anxiety, fear, and worry. It's a tool from God that benefits you in so many ways. That's why the Word of God says:

Then were our mouths filled with laughter, and our tongues with singing. Then they said among the nations, The Lord has done great things for them.

Psalm 126:2

He will yet fill your mouth with laughing, and your lips with rejoicing.

Job 8:21 (NKJV)

A happy heart is good medicine and a cheerful mind works healing, but a broken spirit dries up the bones.

Proverbs 17:22

The Bible says that a happy heart is good medicine because laughter lifts your spirits; improves your mental, emotional, and physical health; and de-stresses your mind. And (here is the best part)... it costs nothing. You've got a proven, God-given weapon against stress that is free of charge and that you can use at any time, day or night.

The Medical Benefits of Laughter

It doesn't matter if it's a night of raucous laughter with hilarious friends, the enjoyment of a funny movie with your family, or even just a giggle over a silly joke—all laughter is a form of stress-relief. It is a physical activity that has nearly unparalleled short-term and long-term benefits for your entire body.

In the short-term, laughter acts as an energizer to your internal organs. It elevates your input of oxygen-rich air; it stimulates your heart, lungs, and muscles; and it boosts the endorphins that are released by your brain. Not only that, but laughter also has been proven to relieve your immediate stress response. Laughter can relax you even in the most anxious situations because it stimulates blood circulation and aids in muscle relaxation. All of these benefits assist in reducing the short-term symptoms of stress.[2]

The long-term gains of laughter are just as beneficial for your body, if not more so. Laughter has been shown to boost your immune system, act as a natural painkiller, lessen depression, and increase personal satisfaction. Negative thoughts can produce chemical reactions that increase stress levels in your body, but laughter and positivity release neuropeptides that battle stress and physical illness. Laughter has been shown to discontinue the pain-spasm cycle seen in muscle disorders and to even benefit people experiencing chronic depression.[3]

If you are not making a decision to laugh on a regular basis, you are missing out on a natural remedy that helps decrease stress and fight against infirmities.

So, the question becomes, *Why aren't we laughing more?* Because the truth is everyone loves to laugh. Charlie Chaplin said that "a day without laughter is a day wasted."[4] And if laughter has the added benefit of

If you are not making a decision to laugh on a regular basis, you are missing out on a natural remedy that helps decrease stress and fight against infirmities.

being such a valuable tool in the battle against worry and anxiety, why aren't we utilizing it each and every day in our homes, at our jobs, and in our churches?

I think there are three answers to that question: (1) Many people just aren't aware of the advantages of joy, happiness, and laughter; (2) we too quickly focus on the negative things in life rather than the positive things—the blessings God has provided; and (3) because of the hectic pace of our routines and the overall busyness we face, we simply overlook our natural opportunities to laugh and enjoy life.

I know it's easy to overlook opportunities to laugh because it's happened to me. I'm a very task-oriented, diligent, business-minded person, and sometimes I can get so focused on the tasks before me that I can be all work and no play. Over the years, God has taught me to take moments to relax and laugh a little, even if it means laughing at my own mistakes.

I remember there were a few months when every time I wore white pants, I spilled coffee on myself.

Literally, *every* time. Obviously I wasn't very happy about it, but I had a choice to make. After it happened for what seemed like the tenth time, I could have gotten furious with myself and called myself a klutz, or I simply could have laughed at the situation and tried to be more careful the next time. I mean, when I stopped and thought about it, it really was ridiculously funny. I guess I either needed to not wear white pants, or I needed to not drink coffee while I was wearing them.

We all have things like this happen, and we all have a choice to either laugh it off or store it up with all the other things that frustrate us in a day's activities. Have you ever had anyone say to you when you were upset over some little thing, "You just need to laugh it off"? That means you can get rid of the frustration and aggravation by just laughing. If we would laugh off more little things, maybe we wouldn't eventually explode from the stress we've stored up throughout the day as we became more and more tense. God may laugh at the things that frustrate us and think, *Seriously . . . you are NOT going to get upset over that little thing, are you?*

I would not want to count the times in my life that I have let some silly, insignificant, and minor irritation ruin my day. Even if we allow them to ruin an hour, or as little as five minutes, it is a foolish choice. Why not try the "laugh it off" therapy and discover for yourself that it works!

It has taken a while, but with God's help, I've learned not to take everything in life so seriously. It's important for me to make time each day to have some fun and take advantage of every opportunity I have to laugh. This is vital in battling the stresses and worries that try to find their way into my life. And the same is true for you. Whether it's something as silly as spilling coffee or something as serious as a major life decision, if you decide to lighten up a little and not take everything too seriously, you'll be surprised at how quickly it will decrease your stress levels.

You might be reading this and thinking, *Joyce, I'd love to laugh more, but I wouldn't know where to begin. I've got too many stressful things to deal with. I don't have anything to laugh about!* Maybe you think you don't have time to laugh because you have so many problems to deal with. If so, I want to encourage you to have an attitude shift today. Rather than thinking you don't have time to laugh, begin to realize you don't have time *not* to laugh. It's vital to your health, your relationships, your inner peace, and your fight

> *Rather than thinking you don't have time to laugh, begin to realize you don't have time not to laugh.*

against stress. Let me offer a few suggestions to help you incorporate a little laughter into your daily life…

How to Laugh on Purpose

One of the most valuable things I have learned in life is that I don't have to wait to *feel* like doing something before I can do it, and neither do you. You can actually learn how to create opportunities for laughter.

- **Plan to laugh...and then do it:** Have you ever scheduled time to be happy? I know it sounds strange at first, but you probably make time in your schedule for other important things—doctor's appointments, school functions, lunch meetings. Why not schedule some laughter? Take a few minutes each day to step away from the busyness and think about the good things that have happened that day. Even if it is not enough to make you laugh out loud, you might at least smile, and even that is helpful. Focus on something funny that a friend said or something enjoyable that you're looking forward to. Don't let stressful events get every minute of your day—schedule time for a little fun.

    My daughter called me last night and told me to watch something on television that was funny, and although I was busy doing something else, I decided to take time to do it. After

I watched it, I called her back and we laughed a long time, talking to one another about the show we had seen. Today I have thought of it several times and it has made me chuckle each time.

When I am waiting in the grocery store for Dave to pay for the groceries, I often go to the greeting card rack and look at the funny birthday cards. I know I will get a good laugh because some of them are hilarious!

- **Hang around funny and encouraging people:** I love to spend time with people who can be lighthearted and encouraging. Their humor and their positive nature are infectious. I'm sure you would agree. It feels a hundred times better to hang around friends who can encourage you and make you laugh than to spend time with people who are going to discourage you and make you feel miserable about your day. If you're dealing with a lot of stress and pressure in your life, one of the most practical things you can do is find some encouraging friends who can make you laugh and spend as much time with them as possible. Sure, there will be many times when you'll have serious conversations with good friends, but having someone in your life who can alleviate stress with some well-timed humor is invaluable.

A couple that works for us travels with us. Pennie is my executive assistant and Mike is our staff pastor. Mike happens to be a person who can be funny without even trying very hard. When our conferences are over and we are headed home after three days of working hard, I can always depend on him for some good laughter.

- **Change your perspective:** One of the best ways to be joyful in life is to begin each day with a "think session." Instead of letting the events of the day shape your perspective, take a few minutes and determine to let the Word of God shape your perspective. Start your morning by deciding to think about some happy, joyful things…on purpose. Then spend some time thinking about Scriptures that are joy-filled (for example, Romans 15:13, Philippians 4:4, Romans 14:17, Psalm 16:9, Proverbs 10:28, 1 Thessalonians 5:16). If you change your perspective—looking for the best things in life rather than the worst things—it's amazing how easy it is to laugh and enjoy life.

> *Start your morning by deciding to think about some happy, joyful things… on purpose.*

- **Rent or download a funny movie:** When I have some downtime, I love to relax in front of a good movie. And a good, clean comedy is a great way to reduce stress. When was the last time you actually sat down in front of a funny movie and just laughed for a couple of hours? Remember, "a happy heart is good medicine," so something as simple as watching your favorite funny movie can be therapeutic for your soul.

- **Laugh at yourself:** I know you are probably very busy, and I'm sure there are many important things you accomplish over the course of an average day, but if you're anything like me, you probably make some pretty amusing mistakes, too. One of the best things you can do when you make a mistake is to laugh about it. I'm not suggesting you don't try to do your best, but once a mistake is made, you can't undo it. Instead, use it to your advantage. Laugh about the silliness of it, learn from it, and move on. One of the reasons people refuse to laugh at themselves is because of insecurities and a low feeling of self-worth. They find their worth in what they do or what others think about them, so when they mess up, they see themselves as a failure in life. But if you're confident in who you are in Christ—knowing that your worth is found in Him and His love for you—no mistake or opinion of another person can keep you from confidently being able to laugh at yourself every once in a while.

I laugh at myself often. For example:

I have caught myself looking frantically for my phone while talking on it.

I have called someone and forgotten whom I called and had to ask, "Who am I talking to?"

One time I went to get a massage and somehow I lost my pants while I was there; they had to give me a pair from the gift shop to go home in!

And this is a very small selection of the things I've done that I can either laugh at or let them make me feel inferior. I choose laughter!!!!

- **Ask God to give you your joy back:** I saved the most important one for last, but that doesn't mean this is the last thing you should do. In fact, this is the first thing you can do in order to live a happy, joy-filled life. In Psalm 51:12, David prayed, "Restore to me the joy of Your salvation." In a very difficult time in David's life, he understood that only God could return his joy. This is true for me and you, too. If you are dealing with painful or demanding circumstances that have sapped you of your joy, taken away your laughter, and brought stress into your life, don't try to go through it alone. Ask God for His help, and ask Him to return

His joy to your heart. He is willing and able to give you "the oil of joy instead of mourning, the garment [expressive] of praise instead of a heavy, burdened, and failing spirit" (Isaiah 61:3).

The Connection between Joy and Laughter

As we end this chapter, take a moment to think about how you've been approaching life. Do you find yourself just trying to make it through the day? Do you commonly deal with stress-induced headaches? If you were honest with yourself, could you even remember the last time you had a good laugh? Well, I want you to know that the joy of the Lord can ease any emotional and physical pain and bring you a new level of satisfaction in life.

The joy of the Lord can ease any emotional and physical pain and bring you a new level of satisfaction in life.

Joy can be anything from a calm delight to an extreme hilarity. On most days, joyful people live in the stage of calm delight, but the times of extreme hilarity have their value, too, and they add so much to life. I once heard someone say that laughter is like internal jogging, and I think that is so true. Laughter improves emotional and mental health, it lifts our spirits, and it dispels worry. It's almost impossible to be anxious and laughing at the same time. This is why we would be wise to express joy in laughter every chance we get. Laughter is the outward evidence of inward joy and it is proven to make you feel better.

One thing is for sure—there is not much chance of laughter if you don't start with a simple smile. Many times I say that some people who are believers need to notify their faces. Instead of smiling, they're frowning; instead of laughing, they're crying. Some Christians are so sour-faced, they look as if they were baptized in lemon juice. But as followers of Jesus, we can be different from the discouraged and depressed around us. The Word of God says that we are the light of the world (see Matthew 5:14). Imagine that your smile is the switch to turn that light on.

You don't have to depend on circumstances or other people for joy. I know that's true because I can be all by myself and smile. I don't even need a reason. It just makes me feel happier to smile occasionally.

If I'm walking around with a frown on my face, it almost always begins to bring me down emotionally. My frown translates to my emotions and disposition. But when I smile, I sense an entire lifting of my countenance. You should try it. Frown for a second and see how you feel . . . okay, now smile and see how *that* feels. Notice the difference?

Maybe you haven't laughed—I mean really laughed—in a very long time. If that is the case, it's probably causing much of the stress you are experiencing today. You will find that you feel better all over after a hearty laugh. Sometimes I feel clean and refreshed after a good laugh. If I am tired and weary from dealing with life's issues, I often feel like my soul is a dusty closet—stale and in need of fresh air. But when I take the opportunity to have a really good laugh, it seems to "air my soul out," refreshing me and lifting the load off my tired mind.

You may be thinking, *Well, Joyce, I don't have anything to laugh about!* Many times I don't either, but that is where the list we discussed in this chapter comes in handy. Use that list and decide to laugh every day as much as possible. When you do, you'll be amazed at how differently you will begin to view your job, your family, your relationships, yourself, and even your walk with God. You'll become a person whose first response to stressful situations is faith not fear, joy not sorrow. You'll be a person like Freddie...

One day the schoolteacher scolded young Freddie, saying, "Freddie, you mustn't laugh out loud in the schoolroom." Freddie responded respectfully by saying, "Sorry, Teacher. I didn't mean to. I was smiling and my smile busted."

That's my prayer for you. My prayer is that no matter what you are going through in life, you will remember the joy of the Lord is your strength. You'll have a smile on your face no matter how intimidating the incident, how stressful the situation, or how discouraging the dilemma. And when things get tough, when you feel like giving up, I pray that your smile will bust. We don't laugh about our problems, but thankfully we can laugh as we trust God to take care of them.

Things to Remember:

➤ Like a wasted vacation day, laughter is an unused benefit if you don't utilize it.

➤ The Word of God says, "A happy heart is good medicine and a cheerful mind works healing, but a broken spirit dries up the bones" (Proverbs 17:22).

➤ Laughter acts as an energizer to your internal organs. It elevates your input of oxygen-rich air; it stimulates your heart, lungs, and muscles; and it boosts the endorphins that are released by your brain.

➤ Laughter has been shown to boost your immune system, act as a natural painkiller, lessen depression, and increase personal satisfaction.

➤ Rather than being passive, sitting around waiting for something to happen, you can choose to laugh, regardless of your circumstances.

➤ The joy of the Lord can be anything from calm delight to extreme hilarity.

➤ With God's help, you can become a person whose first response is faith not fear, joy not sorrow.

KEEP
CALM
AND
BE SECURE

SIMPLE WAYS TO DE-STRESS:

- ✓ Take a deep breath
- ✓ Listen to praise and worship music
- ✓ Go to bed on time (maybe even a little early)
- ✓ Reduce your debt
- ✓ Forgive someone who hurt you
- ✓ Take frequent breaks from your work
- ✓ Be playful and laugh a lot
- ✓ Learn to say no to time demands that will stress you out
- ✓ Eat more fruit and vegetables
- ✓ Plan a fun night out
- ✓ Make a list of things you're thankful for

CHAPTER 9

The Stress of Comparison

*It is not how much we have, but how much we
enjoy that makes happiness.*

—Charles Spurgeon

I wonder what it was like that day. Was it bright
and sunny, or were the clouds threatening? Did
the winds stay calm and quiet, or did they howl in
anticipation for the battle at hand? And what about
the soldiers—did the armies fear the consequences
awaiting them, or were they just anxious to get the
long-awaited fight over with?

Regardless of the weather or the temperament of
the battle-hardened men, here's one thing we know:
In the moments before David fought Goliath...
everyone was waiting. It doesn't sound very exciting, but it's true. Two opposing, well-trained, blood-
thirsty armies stood perched on the opposite sides of
the Valley of Elah as a defiant shepherd boy tried to
do the unthinkable...fit into the armor of a king.

What a sight it must have been for those close
enough to observe—David, a teenage sheepherder,

trying on the stately armor that was custom-made for King Saul. It wasn't David's idea. He hadn't requested the fitting. He didn't want to waste time; David wanted to fight. But the moment David volunteered to battle the giant, those around him began to do what many of us still do today…compare him to another.

Can't you just hear them now? *David, if you're going to fight, you should look the part…If you're going into the valley, wear what an experienced warrior would wear…Walk taller…Act more noble…Look less like a shepherd boy…Look more like a king…Be less like you…Be more like Saul.*

As you read those words, you may be able to relate. You haven't fought a literal giant, but I bet you've battled some giant problems. And perhaps you know what it's like to feel the pressure to dress, look, or act like someone else as you go through life. If you have, let me remind you of the rest of the story.

The comparisons came rolling in, and for a moment, David almost fell into the comparison trap. 1 Samuel 17:38–39 says, "Then Saul clothed David with his armor; he put a bronze helmet on his head and clothed him with a coat of mail. And David girded his sword over his armor." Even though David had never worn armor before, he was tempted to put on Saul's—he was tempted to try to fight like someone else.

But better judgment took over. Verse 39 goes on to say, "Then he tried to go, but could not, for he was not used to it. And David said to Saul, 'I cannot go with these, for I am not used to them.' And David took them off." It's that last sentence that caught my attention. Five simple words that may just be the key to lessening the stress levels in your life: "And David took them off."

David took off the armor...
David took off the expectations of other people...
David took off the comparisons...

And that was the key to his victory. David didn't need to fight like Saul to defeat the giant before him. He simply needed to be himself. All he needed was his slingshot, a few stones, and a confident expectation in God to win the battle. It defied all logic, but God had already given David the unique skills and ability to win the battle. No matter how hard others tried to get David to fight like Saul, the most important thing David could do was to be himself. And you know what? That's the most important thing you can do, too.

> No matter how hard others tried to get David to fight like Saul, the most important thing David could do was to be himself.

An Eagle's Feather

One of the most common sources of stress is the comparison trap. This isn't just anecdotally true;

studies have borne this out. One study published in the *Quarterly Journal of Economics* found that "the higher earnings of neighbors were associated with lower levels of self-reported happiness."[1] For so many people, happiness is connected to the comparison of those around them.

> *The more you compare your life to those around you, the less you'll enjoy the life God has given you.*

But I've discovered that nothing good comes from trying to imitate, compete with, or outdo someone else. The more you compare your life to those around you, the less you'll enjoy the life God has given you. Billy Graham said it this way: "I defy you to show me an envious man who is a happy man."[2] If you think about it, this is so true. The more you look at the people around you and try to live a life different from your own, the less happy you become.

Even though we would all probably agree that comparison is a bad idea, it is a mistake that so many people make. And I can certainly relate. I've fallen into the comparison trap many times myself—more times than I'd like to admit. I can still remember the times I wanted to be more like my neighbor who was an amazing homemaker and cook, or to be like the sweet, mercy-motivated woman I knew from church, or more like Dave, who is so easygoing in how he handles life. The temptation to measure myself against others is one that I've struggled with many times.

But over the years, the Lord has shown me that the only thing that comes from comparison is stress. God didn't create me to be like someone else, so why should I try to be anything other than what I am? As a matter of fact, the things that make me unique are gifts, not liabilities. I'll give you an example...

For the longest time, I wondered why I had such a deep voice. I mean, honestly, there were times I was really upset about it. Other ladies had such soft, gentle tones and I wondered why I couldn't have the same. (There was one time when I called for a facial and the person on the other end of the line thought I was a man! I thought, *How embarrassing!*) But over the years, God has shown me that He gave me this voice on purpose—I need it to boldly proclaim the Word of God all around the world! He gave me a unique gift that I can use for His glory.

The same is true for you. The things in your life that make you different aren't hindrances...they are assets. That's why Psalm 139:14 (NKJV) says:

> *The things in your life that make you different aren't hindrances...they are assets.*

I will praise You, for I am fearfully and wonderfully made;

Marvelous are Your works,
And that my soul knows very well.

You are handcrafted—fearfully and wonder-fully made! Just like David, God has specially and uniquely qualified you to do something that no one else can do. You might be thinking, *But, Joyce, I don't know what that is yet!* Just because you haven't discovered it yet doesn't mean you won't. Stay encouraged. God has something specific planned for your future! Resist the temptation to compare yourself to other people. Trust God and allow Him to use you in ways that are unique to you.

Dwight L. Moody once told the story of a beautiful eagle who was jealous of another eagle who seemed to fly better than he could. One day the wild bird saw a hunter with a bow and arrow and said to him, "I wish you would bring down that eagle up there." The man said he gladly would if he just had some feathers for his arrow. So, of course, the envious eagle pulled one out of his wing. The arrow was shot, but it didn't quite reach the rival bird because he was flying so high. The envious eagle pulled out another feather…and then another…and then another—until he had lost so many that he himself couldn't fly. The sportsman took advantage of the situation, turned around, and killed the helpless bird. And here is the application that D. L. Moody made: If you are jealous of others, the one you will hurt the most will be yourself.[3]

True Security and Freedom from Comparisons

We have an epidemic of insecure people in our society today. Many people have an identity crisis because they don't really know who they are, and they base their worth and value on all the wrong things—what they do, what they look like, who they know, what they know, or what they own.

Let me ask you a few questions. What do you think of yourself? How do you feel about who you are? Do you ever compare yourself with other people and feel belittled if you can't do what they can do or be like them? Have you ever said, "I wish I looked like her," or "I wish I had what they have," or "I wish I could do what you do"? If you have, don't beat yourself up—everyone experiences insecurity at times. I know what it's like to feel inferior to others and insecure about myself. I grew up in a very unstable, volatile home environment and never really felt safe and secure throughout my childhood. I suffered for many years with the agony of trying to be someone other than myself, but I learned that wasn't God's will. Theodore Roosevelt said, "Comparison is the thief of joy."[4] The more you are comfortable with *you*, the more joy you will have.

The good news is, we don't have to live insecure lives because it's God's will for us to be very secure and not to live in fear. We were created to feel safe, secure, confident, and bold; it's part of our spiritual DNA as born-again believers in Christ. But the key to living a secure life in Christ is knowing who you are in Christ, really receiving God's love for you, and basing your worth and value on who God says you are, not what you do.

I remember my first speaking engagement, when I was to speak in front of several hundred people. All the other guest speakers had impressive titles. They were doctors, reverends, bishops, and theologians, but I was just Joyce. I felt extremely insecure. Fast-forward thirty years to when I was recently part of a conference where the other speakers were some of the most revered men in Christian circles. I'm talking about really important men with loads of major influence. There were these prestigious speakers and then there was me! But you know what? I didn't feel one tiny bit insecure because I knew from my thirty-plus years of experience with God that I don't have to compare myself with anyone. We are equal to any task God assigns us as long as we keep our confidence in Him.

Any time we try to do something that God has not given us an ability to do, we are inviting stress into our lives. The pressure we can feel when we are

with people that we feel
threatened by can be very
stressful. It causes us to
behave unnaturally or in a
way that is not a true representation of how we really

Any time we try to do something that God has not given us an ability to do, we are inviting stress into our lives.

are. It is difficult, if not impossible, to form healthy
relationships with anyone we are constantly comparing ourselves to.

According to Isaiah 54:17, part of our inheritance
from God is security: "But no weapon that is formed
against you shall prosper, and every tongue that shall
rise against you in judgment you shall show to be in
the wrong. This [peace, righteousness, **security**, triumph over opposition] is the heritage of the servants
of the Lord" (emphasis added).

I think stress is a certainty unless we have a deep
understanding that God loves us unconditionally. In
1 John 4:18, it says, "There is no fear in love...but
full grown (complete, perfect) love turns fear out of
doors and expels every trace of terror!"

This Scripture opened my eyes to the fact that I
was one of those people who didn't feel secure in God's
love. To be loved unconditionally means that the love
we receive isn't based on what we do. God's love is
perfect and it is a free gift. I've had to remind myself at
times that I am not *Joyce Meyer Ministries*. I am a person who is in ministry. You are more than your job, or

education level, or even your talent and abilities. We are God's very own; we belong to Him and He loves us UNCONDITIONALLY!! God is love. And He really loves you! I pray that you will experience God's love for yourself every day of your life. Then you can have the life of peace, joy, and true security that He's planned for you. I once heard that comparison is an act of violence against yourself, and I agree. Be kind to yourself and appreciate who you are.

This, Not That

Let's end this chapter with some practical ways to avoid the stress that comes with comparing yourself with others. All of these might not apply to your life, but I encourage you to implement the ones that do on a daily basis. It may take time—and you might fall short on some days—but don't give up. Each day, ask the Lord to help you look to Him and recognize His love for you. Rather than finding your identity by comparing yourself with another, ask God to help you confidently find your identity in Him.

Here are some helpful ways to remember that each and every day...

- When you see someone else who has an amazing gift, instead of being jealous, take a moment to thank God for their ability, and realize that their gift benefits you if you will enjoy it instead of being jealous of it.

- Begin by asking God to give you a new confidence in who He has gifted you to be.
- Realize that things about you that are unique are not liabilities, but they are actually resources that God can use.
- Instead of trying to copy someone else's talent, work on developing your own talent. What is it that you can do that others cannot? Whatever that thing is...cultivate it. Strengthen your strengths and trust that God gave you those talents for a reason.
- Pray for your friends, coworkers, and neighbors. Regardless of their status or behavior, ask God to bless them each and every day. It's really difficult to be envious of those people you are praying for. If you ask God to bless others, you might be surprised at how much He'll bless you in return.

So, once and for all, let's climb out of the pit of comparisons and walk in the freedom of our identity in Christ. David "took off" the armor of Saul that held him down...and you and I can do the same. We can take off the things that have burdened us in the past. Whether it's the way you look, how you dress, your marital status, what job you have, the level of your education, the size of your home, or the depth of your talent, remember that you are "fearfully and wonderfully made." Don't allow the stress of comparisons to reign in your life. Take them off and allow God to give you a level of peace and joy that can propel you into your destiny.

Things to Remember:

➤ David set the example by fighting the battle using the unique gifts and skill sets God had given him.

➤ Nothing good comes from trying to imitate, compete with, or outdo someone else. The more you compare your life to the lives of those around you, the less you'll enjoy the life God has given you.

➤ Psalm 139:14 (NKJV) says, "I will praise You, for I am fearfully and wonderfully made; marvelous are Your works, and that my soul knows very well."

➤ We were created to feel safe, secure, confident, and bold; these are part of our spiritual DNA as born-again believers in Christ.

➤ God created you with a purpose. He loves you unconditionally, and He has given you special gifts and talents.

Did you know?

People who own dogs are less likely to experience stress on the same level as people who do not.[5]

KEEP
CALM
AND
WATCH WHAT
YOU SAY

CHAPTER 10

Change the Conversation

Good words are worth much, and cost little.
—George Herbert

Do you remember the first words your child spoke? *Mama. Dada. Ball. Dog.* Nothing is more exciting than hearing a baby talk for the first time. We call our friends, brag on Facebook, and post videos on Instagram. (You know it's true.) And we spend the next few weeks begging our little one to say it again. I have spent two weeks trying to get my one-year-old grandson to say anything that even remotely sounds like *grandma*! Words can lift us into ecstasy or they can cause some of the worst emotional pain we can feel as humans. Right words at the right time are very valuable.

> Words can lift us into ecstasy or they can cause some of the worst emotional pain we can feel as humans.

But can you imagine if your child's first words were something critical or negative? What if your son or daughter started their voyage into language by saying *can't* or *never* or *ugly*? You wouldn't be so quick to run to social media. You wouldn't be proud at all. Why? Because the words your child speaks are foundational and show what's important in his life. You, rightfully, want your little child to speak positive things that bring him joy and fulfillment.

Well, what's true for children is true for us, too. The words you and I speak may not cause relatives to grab their phones and instantly flood social media, but they are just as important. As a matter of fact, the words you speak each day are an indication of the kind of life you are going to live. If your conversations are positive, hope-filled, and full of encouragement, you are going to face that day with a certain level of joy and optimism. However, if your conversations are despair-riddled, stress-filled, and burdened by doubt, you are probably in for a long day...a very long, stressful day.

This is why I believe it's time to "change the conversation." Rather than rehearse your problems, it's time to start reciting God's goodness! In my life, I've seen that talking excessively about my cares or concerns does nothing to make them go away. All talking about my problems does is maximize stress. I can feel the tension getting worse the longer I talk. The more I talk about everything that could go wrong, the more I am turning up the volume on stress and turning down the volume on faith. But something amazing happens when I change the conversation. When I begin talking about the power, the goodness, and the faithfulness of God (in spite of my problems), or when I talk about parts of my life that are not problems, my stress levels decrease. It's not that my words instantly change the circumstances I'm facing, but they have the power to change my attitude about those circumstances until the circumstances do change.

Change your conversation! Rather than stressing out about what is lacking, talk about how fortunate you are in many areas of life. It's a simple solution to the nagging problem of stress: worry can be lessened by speaking positive, hope-inspired, and faith-filled words.

How to Increase Your Joy

There is no doubt you have heard someone say, "You might end up eating those words." It may sound like a simple expression to us, but in reality we do eat our words. What we say not only affects our friends and coworkers, but our words also profoundly affect us. The question is which way—positively or negatively?

Words are wonderful when used in a proper way. They can encourage, edify, and give confidence to the hearer. A right word spoken at the right time can actually be life-changing (see Proverbs 15:23).

I wonder how many people who are seriously stressed out ever consider that a large part of it may be caused by their own conversation?

We can literally increase our own joy and greatly reduce stress by speaking right words. We can also upset ourselves by talking unnecessarily about our problems or about things that have hurt us in relationships. I wonder how many people who are seriously stressed out ever consider that a large part of it may be caused by their own conversation?

One time I was dealing with a disappointing situation that took place with someone I considered to be a friend. I noticed that each time I talked about it, I would have a difficult time getting it off my mind for the remainder of the day. I finally realized that if I wanted to get over it and move on, I had to stop mentally and verbally rehearsing it again and again. People kept asking me about the situation out of genuine concern, but I ultimately realized that I had to answer, "It is better for me if I just don't talk about it right now." The more I spoke about it, the greater the opportunity for stress and worry. But when I simply took the situation to God, cast my care upon Him, and quit talking about it, I noticed that my entire attitude began to improve.

Think for a moment about what happens when we verbalize a thought. The words that come out of our mouths go into our own ears (as well as other people's), and then they drop down into our soul where they give us either joy or sadness, peace or stress, depending on the types of words we have spoken. Most people don't realize how helpful or destructive their own words are to their lives. When we understand the power of words and realize that we can choose what we think and speak, our lives can be transformed.

God desires that our spirits be light and free so they can function properly, not heavy and oppressed. We can learn to choose our thoughts, to resist wrong ones, and think about good, healthy, and right ones. I have often said, "Where the mind goes, the man follows." And it could also be said that where the mind goes, the mouth follows!

Plan to Say Something Positive

God has given every believer a new nature, and we are taught to daily renew our mind and attitude. Having a positive outlook on life and speaking words based on God's Word are two of the most essential things we can do in the renewing process. As you begin your day, if there is something on your schedule that you're not looking forward to, you can either say, "I am dreading this day already," or you can say, "God will give me strength today to do whatever I need to do and to do it with joy." Which of these two statements do you think would better prepare you for the day?

As we have seen, we eat our words, and we can rightfully say that they are food for our souls. Anyone who wants to be healthy is careful to choose nutritious, quality food that will provide proper fuel for the body. In the same way, if we want to be healthy in our soul and spirit, we can also choose to take in words that will build us up and increase our peace and joy.

You might be thinking, *But, Joyce, there are so many negative things that are happening all around me.* I know sometimes that seems to be true, but I believe there are many good things happening in the world, and there is probably more good than bad. But the evil is magnified in a way that often seems overwhelming. Turn on any news station or go to any online news site and you will find it filled with reports of murder, theft, wars, famine, and all kinds of terribly tragic events. We want to be well informed of what is going on, but to talk about world problems excessively or with no purpose merely creates a gloomy atmosphere that nobody will enjoy.

I once walked into a room and heard a group of people talking about several businesses that had just filed for bankruptcy. Then they mentioned two others that they had heard were going to file for bankruptcy. I felt a gloom hanging in the atmosphere, so I spoke up and said, "Well, God is not bankrupt and He is on our side." Everyone agreed with me and immediately, the atmosphere changed. I am not suggesting at all that we deny reality, but we can choose what we talk about. Instead of feeding ourselves a steady diet of bad news, we should choose to read, watch, and talk about good things. What we allow into our lives will affect us.

So the question becomes, *What are you talking about?* I ask that because we talk a lot and quite often pay no attention to what we are saying, let alone think seriously about the impact of our words. Someone told me that the chattiest of women speak 47,000 words a day, and average women speak 20,000, while men speak only 7,000. I must admit I'm having a difficult time believing that one because I know some men who can easily keep up with me, but one thing is for sure—we all say lots of things that would be better off left unsaid.

> *Instead of feeding ourselves a steady diet of bad news, we should choose to read, watch, and talk about good things.*

If we are honest with ourselves, we may find that some of our stress, worry, and anxiety are directly linked to our conversations. I urge you to start paying attention to how you feel when you are talking about your problems, things that upset you, or even the world problems we all know exist. Do your muscles become tense? Do you start to grit your teeth? Does your stomach begin to churn? Do you get a headache? These are all symptoms of stress. We all have the solution to stress caused by what we say... change the conversation!

Your words may not be the cause of all your problems, but they can cause a lot of them. It would be helpful to give them a good deal of consideration when you are looking for answers to the stress you encounter in life. We all face challenges from time to time, but we can make them better or worse by the way we talk about them. I don't believe we can change all of our circumstances into pleasant ones by making positive confessions, but I do believe many of them will change according to God's will when we speak according to His will. One thing is for sure—speaking negatively can hurt you and speaking positively never will, so why not go with the positive just to be on the safe side?

Don't Talk Yourself Out of Victory

The Word of God has much to say about the words we choose to speak. And if this is an area in your life where you know you need to make some changes, it would be beneficial for you to see what God says and put His instruction into practice. Here are a few biblical directions and encouragements about our word choices:

> *Let no foul or polluting language, nor evil word nor unwholesome or worthless talk [ever] come out of your mouth, but only such [speech] as is good and beneficial to the spiritual progress of others, as is fitting to the need and the occasion, that it may be a blessing and give grace (God's favor) to those who hear it.*
>
> Ephesians 4:29

> *Let the words of my mouth and the meditation of my heart be acceptable in Your sight, O Lord, my [firm, impenetrable] Rock and my Redeemer.*
>
> Psalm 19:14

> *But I tell you, on the day of judgment men will have to give account for every idle (inoperative, nonworking) word they speak.*
>
> Matthew 12:36

> *Pleasant words are as a honeycomb, sweet to the mind and healing to the body.*
>
> Proverbs 16:24

These are just a few of the many admonishments in the Bible for you and me to "change the conversation." Positive, God-inspired words are "sweet to the mind" and bring "healing to the body."

Are You Talking Too Much?

God has challenged me to "fast my words." In other words, don't talk just to hear myself talk, but refrain from saying useless, vain, and powerless things. I would love to be able to report that I have done great, but the truth is that I am still making *very slow* progress. However, I do want to share that on the days I have been more successful, I actually notice that I feel more relaxed and, at times, I even feel closer to God.

This morning, Dave and I got into a downright silly conversation. I think we started out trying to tease each other, but our conversation digressed into something that sounded more like insults and seemed to be heading for an argument. Later in the day, the same thing happened with one of my sons. I guess since I was the common denominator in both of the conversations, I should take responsibility for it (ouch!). The Bible warns us against "coarse jesting," which is trying to be funny but doing so in a crude or rude manner (see Ephesians 5:4).

I have known several people in my life who can be very funny, but when they are enjoying making everyone laugh, they often move into being rude instead of funny by making jokes about weaknesses or defects that some of the people have who are actually present and part of the conversation. This usually ends up with someone being offended, so it obviously is not a good choice. These are conversations that cause stress and anxiety and are provoked by people talking too much when they truly have nothing good to say. This is the type of talk I had entered into just this morning when I realized my conversation with Dave needed to change.

I saved what could have turned into a day of stress by just changing my conversation, and you can do the same thing. But it would have been even better in both of the situations had I just enjoyed the quiet and not felt the need to fill the air space with silly, useless words. I think it is quite possible to avoid a lot of our stress by just making an effort to not talk unless we truly have something worthy of being said.

> It is quite possible to avoid a lot of our stress by just making an effort to not talk unless we truly have something worthy of being said.

I believe we'll have greater success with this if we concentrate on what we *should* be saying, rather than focusing on all the things we shouldn't say. It's self-defeating to go around saying things like, "I shouldn't do that... I'd better not do this..." It would be better if we took time to be mindful of God's promises and scriptural encouragements. These are the things we can and should say. In 1 Samuel 30:6, when David was distressed, he "encouraged and strengthened" himself in the Lord. We can do the same thing! Here are a few examples from God's Word:

- **Bless everything** you can possibly bless. James 3:8–10 says we have the power to bless or curse with the words of our mouth. Choose to use your words to be a blessing.
- **Be thankful** and say so! (see Psalm 100:4). Don't just think about how much you appreciate someone—tell them! It will make their day...and yours.
- **Be an encourager** (see Hebrews 10:24–25). Make an effort to give someone an encouraging word every day. This is a practice that will change the way you view other people and yourself.
- **Tell the truth!** There is power in truth. Don't listen to, or rehearse, the lies of the enemy. John 8:32 (NKJV) says, "And you shall know the truth, and the truth shall make you free."

Maybe you've never really thought about the words you are speaking each day. Or maybe you've fallen into the habit of rehearsing your problems and speaking negative, discouraging words and didn't even know you were doing it. Whatever the case, I want to encourage you to make a fresh start today. It's never too late to change your conversation. Use the effective tool God has given you to battle stress: your words.

Things to Remember:

➤ You can actually talk yourself out of being joyful by using careless or reckless words.
➤ You can talk yourself into stress.
➤ Rather than rehearse your problems, it's time to start reciting God's goodness!
➤ Pleasant words are as a honeycomb, sweet to the mind and healing to the body (Proverbs 16:24).
➤ Talking too much can disturb our peace and cause stress.

Did you know?

When cells shrink due to exposure to stress hormones, they disconnect from one another, which contributes to depression.[1]

KEEP
CALM
AND
ENJOY THE
JOURNEY

CHAPTER 11

It Is Well with My Soul

Half of our life is spent trying to find something to do with the time we have rushed through life trying to save.

—Will Rogers

When I first felt the leading of God to go into ministry, I started right away by teaching Bible studies, then working for a church, and then starting Joyce Meyer Ministries. I believed then (and by God's grace, time has proven) it was God's will for me to do those things. But when I first started ministering, I didn't know the spiritual principles to decrease stress that we're talking about in this book. And because of that, I nearly burned myself out and most of the time was not enjoying what I was doing. People are often surprised to hear that, but it's true. There were many days I was just plain miserable.

Back in those days, my husband, Dave, did something that absolutely drove me crazy. It wasn't a typical annoyance that wives often complain about. Dave didn't throw his socks on the floor or leave his dishes sitting in the sink. To me, it was way more obnoxious than that—Dave enjoyed his life. He was always happy! I remember thinking, *I'm miserable, frustrated, and upset—Dave should be, too!* But no matter how grouchy I acted, how busy we became, or what challenges we faced, Dave was determined to stay joyful. He would tell me (and still reminds me today), "Joyce, just cast your care. God's got everything under control." And then he would put a smile on his face and go out and actually enjoy his day. *How dare he!*

I kid about that, but the truth is that Dave's attitude was a great example to me. He showed me that we can choose to be joyful…we can choose to be content…we can choose to love life regardless of the circumstances around us. The more I watched Dave decide to love his life, the more I recognized that he wasn't nearly as stressed as I was. We could be going through the same situation but have totally different attitudes and mind-sets. Mine normally involved a lot of stress, but his never did. Now, it's true that our personalities are different, but this was something bigger than simple personality quirks—Dave was making a conscious

> *We can choose to be joyful…we can choose to be content…we can choose to love life regardless of the circumstances around us.*

effort to enjoy each day of his life. That was a great revelation to me. Peace and happiness are choices we get to make! And, believe it or not, we can decide whether we want to be stressed out or not!

That may sound like a foreign concept to you, especially if you are dealing with a traumatic situation or an overwhelming obstacle, but I want you to know that you don't have to be a victim of your circumstances. No matter how minor or major the stress you are facing, it is only part of your journey. It will eventually pass and things will get better.

Philippians 4:4 says, "Rejoice in the Lord always [delight, gladden yourselves in Him]; again I say, Rejoice!" The apostle Paul wrote that verse while in prison, and the prisons in his day were worse than anything we could imagine. One of the key words in that verse is the word *always*. Rain or shine, good day or bad, when you're on the mountaintop or in the valley, you can *always* rejoice. God's promises aren't dependent on what's happening around us; He gives us hope and goodness to rejoice about every single day. While we are going through something difficult, we can rejoice that we are *going through*, and not stuck forever.

In this chapter, I want to address three questions that I'm often asked and you may be dealing with: (1) How can I be responsible for my own happiness?

(2) Can I be content when I still have a long way to go? (3) Is it possible to enjoy life even in the midst of deep pain? If you're ready to put fear, worry, stress, and anxiety in their place and take back control of your life, keep reading. I think this chapter is going to really help you.

How to Be Responsible for My Own Happiness

Which of these attitudes do you have most mornings? Do you greet each day with an aggressive, expectant, positive attitude about what the day holds, or do you feel like pulling the blankets over your head, dreading what awaits you outside your front door?

We can combat the dread that tempts us to stay in bed by keeping a positive attitude and mind-set. Our attitude is so important in determining how we view each day. Our level of joy is, to a great degree, shaped by our thoughts and actions. If we dwell on negative attitudes, expecting the worst, our actions will reflect those thoughts. Dread is a close relative of fear, and allowing it to remain in your mind sets you up for misery and robs you of joy. In order to enjoy your life, it is essential to give special attention to your attitude. You are not just the victim of circumstances, and you must take responsibility for your joy if you ever truly want to have it.

Once, I experienced a feeling of dread as we were planning a trip to speak in India. Don't get me wrong, I was excited about the wonderful opportunity there, but I kept thinking about the long flight, the extremely hot weather, and the poor conditions that exist in that country. I'm grateful that I knew how to dispel those negative feelings with positive thoughts about what could be accomplished during our time there. If I had allowed myself to dwell on the negative aspects of the trip, it would've taken away the joy and excitement God wanted me to experience and potentially limit my effectiveness. Dread is a thief of joy! Dread is a trap, but you can be determined not to fall into it. If not being sure of the future or facing new things causes you to feel dread or fear, remember Philippians 4:13 says, "I am ready for anything and equal to anything through Him Who infuses inner strength into me."

Enjoying life begins with enjoying yourself. You're the one person you're never going to get away from, so you'd better learn to like yourself. It's impossible to love your life if you don't love yourself. We have a well of wonderful things on the inside of us, and no matter what's going on around us, we can find joy in holding on to the hope that is ours in Jesus.

There'll always be roadblocks that try to keep us from enjoying the life God has provided for us. With all the stress and pressures of everyday life, we

You can choose to be in control, instead of letting your circumstances control you.

must make a decision that we're going to enjoy life regardless of our circumstances. Every single day is filled with all kinds of situations that could upset you—like losing your car keys or having an appliance break—but you can choose to be in control, instead of letting your circumstances control you.

Control Yourself, Not Other People

We can make our days stressful by trying to control what everyone does. There was a time when I got upset and felt sorry for myself for days when Dave wanted to play golf. I didn't play golf and I didn't want Dave to play. I was being selfish and didn't realize that it was a way for Dave to relax. I just wanted to control everything and make it to my liking. If you are like I was, this is a great time to face it and ask God to help you make a change. It is time to control yourself instead of other people.

It is not God's will for any of us to control another individual. He wants each of us to be led and guided by the Holy Spirit. We can express our preferences if we do so unselfishly, but we must not try to manipulate and control. Doing so is one of the major causes of stress in relationships and can ultimately cause divorce if not corrected.

You can enjoy freedom in your life! Being free—and allowing others to do the same—is a healthy and positive approach to life that pleases God. If you are in a relationship with someone who tries to control you, it will be necessary for your sake and theirs to confront them in a firm but godly way. I grew up being controlled by my father, and all I remember from those years is stress and fear. These enemies stole my childhood, and I want to help make sure that they don't steal your joy in life moving forward. Thankfully, I learned to give Dave freedom and he does the same for me. It brings peace into our relationship and helps us enjoy our journey through life.

How You Can Be Content When You Still Have a Long Way to Go

The expression "nobody's perfect" is used or heard almost every day, and it's true—I'm not perfect, you're not perfect, nobody's perfect. Hopefully, though, we're all getting better and are on our way toward the goals God has given us. The important thing to remember is that even though we're not yet perfect, we're still okay. Just because we haven't arrived yet doesn't mean that we're not on our way, and that is what we can rejoice in, even if we still have a long way to go.

It's true that we all have a long way to go in different areas of our lives. I used to get discouraged about how far I had to go, and it seemed like I was reminded of it every day (sometimes every hour). For many years, I carried a nagging sense of failure—a feeling that I just wasn't who I needed to be, I wasn't doing enough, and I needed to try harder. But when I did try harder, I only failed again.

I've now adopted a new attitude: "I'm not where I need to be, but thank God I'm not where I used to be. I'm okay, and I'm on my way!" I now know with all my heart that God isn't angry with me just because I haven't arrived yet. He's pleased that I'm pressing on and staying on the path. And the same is true for you! If you and I will just "keep on keeping on," God will be pleased with our desire to please Him.

Keep moving forward by simply walking the walk one step at a time. This is an important thing to remember. It's true that we have to keep pressing on, but thank God we don't have to hate or reject ourselves while we're trying to get to our destination. You don't have to be stressed by how far you still have to go—all you need to do is keep going. If I invited you to take a walk, you'd think I was crazy if I became angry after the first few steps because we

hadn't yet arrived at our destination. We can understand ordinary things like this, yet we have a difficult time understanding that God expects it to take
some time for us to grow spiritually. We should keep
this in mind not only concerning ourselves, but also
when it comes to our attitudes and dealings with
other people.

The process can be difficult. Growing and learning are never easy, but the changes make us better
people. We begin to think differently, then to talk
differently, and finally, to act differently. This process develops in stages, and we must always remember that while it's taking place, we can have an "I'm
okay, and I'm on my way!" attitude. It is tragic not to
enjoy our journey through life. We only get one life
and we should maximize it!

So, enjoy yourself while you're changing, growing, and becoming more like Christ. Enjoy where
you are on the way to where you're going. Enjoy the
journey! Don't waste all of your "now time" trying
to rush into the future. Remember, tomorrow will
have troubles of its own (see Matthew 6:34).

It's important to remember that you can be extraor-
dinarily happy while living an ordinary, everyday
life. Expecting life to be one long series of exciting
events is setting yourself up for disappointment—
and that'll increase stress and steal your joy! So

decide to be content and live life as it comes. At our house we call it "going with the flow." You will enjoy each day only if you decide to. Don't wait for joyful feelings, but first make a decision and feelings will follow in due time. Start your days by saying, "This is the day the Lord has made. I *will* rejoice and be glad in it. Good morning, Lord!" (See Psalm 118:24.)

Today you may be wrestling with anger, fear, or bitterness, thinking if you could be free in this area, everything would be all right. But the truth is, we are all usually dealing with something. We overcome one thing only to find another thing has taken its place and we are back in that same frame of mind again, thinking, *If only I didn't have this problem, I could be happy.* We can learn to look at these things in a new way. We can be free to believe that we are, indeed, okay and on our way—not perfected yet, but pressing on. We can be free to enjoy life, enjoy God, and enjoy ourselves. I am now enjoying a lot of victory over things that were once big problems for me, but I am still learning to fast my words, be more patient, be less selfish, and many other things. We don't have to focus on how far we still have to go and let it stress us out and steal our joy. We can celebrate how far we have come! We can enjoy the journey!

How to Enjoy Life Even in the Midst of Deep Pain

Horatio Spafford (1828–1888) was a wealthy Chicago lawyer who had a wife and four precious daughters. Everything seemed to be going great for Spafford. His legal practice was thriving, his family was happy, and, as a strong believer, his circle of friends included D. L. Moody, Ira Sankey, and other well-known ministers of the day.

Though Spafford had made terrific professional and financial gains, he also suffered terrible personal loss. In October 1871, the Great Chicago Fire destroyed nearly every real estate investment he had. But in typical fashion, Horatio didn't get down. He and his wife, Anna, spent the next two years volunteering to help work among the refugees of the fire.

Two years later, devastating tragedy struck. The Spafford family had planned to join friends in Europe for some time away. Just before their departure, Horatio was detained with work. He persuaded Anna and his girls to go ahead without him; he would take another ship and meet them later. But Horatio would never see his daughters again. As his wife and daughters traveled across the Atlantic, the steamship they were traveling on, the *Ville du Havre*, collided with another ship and sank.

Out of the hundreds on board, Anna was one of

only twenty-seven survivors. She was able to stay alive by clinging to floating debris until rescuers arrived. Overcome with sadness, she sent a telegram to Horatio with just two words on it: "Saved alone."

As sad as this story is, there is something amazing about Horatio's response I want you to see. Traveling across the Atlantic Ocean, the watery grave for his four daughters, to join his grieving wife, Horatio Spafford didn't get angry, he didn't give up hope, and he didn't run from God. Instead, he took out pen and paper and wrote a hymn. He penned these familiar words:

When peace like a river attendeth my way
When sorrows like sea billows roll,
Whatever my lot,
Thou hast taught me to say:
It is well, it is well, with my soul

"It Is Well with My Soul" is still one of the most beloved hymns in churches today. What an amazing sentiment. In the most difficult circumstance imaginable, Spafford leaned on God and trusted that things could get better. Sure, he was hurting, and he certainly had suffered loss, but even in the midst of that pain he could say, "It is well with my soul."[1]

I realize that I don't know the depth of your pain today. Perhaps you've suffered an unthinkable loss like Horatio and Anna, or perhaps your trial has been less severe. Whatever you're going through, pain is pain, and I know it can seem overwhelming. Oftentimes when we're hurting, we think it is impossible to enjoy life—not only in the present but also ever again. I've experienced loss and I can relate to that feeling. But here is something I've learned: a struggle or personal loss doesn't have to overshadow every part of your life. You can still have joy even in the midst of sorrow. As we said in a previous chapter, joy isn't always extreme hilarity—sometimes joy is simply a calm delight. And you can delight yourself in God and in His promise to always be with you (see Deuteronomy 31:6) even when times are difficult... *especially* when times are difficult.

The key is to trust. God knows what you're going through, and if you'll trust Him, He will restore your joy. When I get bad news or when things look out of control, I say out loud, "God, I trust You." I may not know how it's going to work out or how I'm going to get over it, but I know God can do the impossible. And then if I get worried or if stress tries to steal my peace, I say it again: "God, I trust You." I've found this is such a helpful exercise. *I trust You...I trust You...I trust You.* I may have to say it twenty times in a row, but it's a reminder to my spirit that God is going to

> God knows what you're going through, and if you'll trust Him, He will restore your joy.

bring something good out of this situation. Romans 8:28 says it this way:

> We are assured and know that [God being a partner in their labor] all things work together and are [fitting into a plan] for good to and for those who love God and are called according to [His] design and purpose.

So I encourage you to trust God today. He knows what you're going through, and He has a plan for your life. No matter what the circumstances may say, God is by your side, and He is going to see you through. Don't get angry, don't give up hope, and don't run from God. Trust Him and allow Him to help you enjoy life, even in the midst of pain.

The Happiness Choice

We started this chapter by talking about how my husband, Dave, makes the choice to enjoy his life regardless of the environment around him. And I want to end it by reminding you that you can do the same thing. You don't have to let stress have the final say. When others around you are fuming, when the situation looks bleak, when the frantic pace of life seems exhausting, you can still say, "I choose to enjoy my day. I choose to enjoy my family. I choose to enjoy my life." It might not seem natural at first, but don't give up. I think sometimes we feel guilty if we are enjoying life while difficulty exists, but we shouldn't. Remember, our joy (enjoyment) is our strength to help us get through the difficulty.

Keep choosing happiness until it becomes second nature. It might annoy the people around you in the beginning—happy people are the exception, not the rule—but eventually they'll come around. They'll admire your determination and follow your example. But, more important, you'll start to feel better. You will definitely have less stress. The daily struggles and pressures of life won't preoccupy your mind anymore. You'll finally be able to enjoy the life Jesus died to give you.

Things to Remember:

➤ Peace and happiness don't happen by accident. These are choices you get to make.
➤ No matter how minor or major the stress you are facing, you can enjoy your life...every single day.
➤ Dread is a close relative of fear, and allowing it to remain in your mind sets you up for misery and robs you of joy. In order to enjoy your life, it is essential to give special attention to your attitude.

➤ Expecting life to be one long series of exciting events is setting yourself up for disappointment—and that'll increase stress and steal your joy.

➤ Trust God in the midst of trying times. He knows what you're going through; He hasn't left you; He has a plan for your life.

Did you know?

The hyper-arousal of the body's stress response system can lead to chronic insomnia.[2]

KEEP
CALM
AND
MAKE SOME
CHANGES

CHAPTER 12

Facing Stress Head-on!

The more things you do, the more you can do.
—Lucille Ball

One of the best things you can do in life is to have a plan. If you're going to make any progress in any area, it is important that you make a plan and then begin to put that plan into action. There will be times when you may have to make adjustments and alterations to your plan as you go (and it is always essential that you submit your plans to God), but you can't have success unless you have planned for it in one way or another.

Imagine if a coach told his team before the big game how important it was that they win because the entire season was riding on this one game—but when asked by his players what the game plan was, he replied, "Well, I don't know. I don't really have a plan. Just try your best." That wouldn't make sense. That coach would be setting his team and himself up for failure.

Or imagine if a mother told her children that

though college was expensive, she insisted they attend when they graduate high school—but when the kids asked how it would be paid for, she said, "Oh, I don't know. Your father and I have never planned for it. But you still have to go." That would be a frustrating and a possibly fearful thing for her kids to deal with. How would they accomplish the task with no plan in place?

Making a plan is an action step, and action is important. We can't sit passively by and just wish that stress would go away. Nothing happens when we take a passive posture. It's important that we are active in our faith if we are going to see spiritual and emotional progress.

With God's help, we can attack stress instead of sitting back, waiting for it to attack us.

That's why I believe, with God's help, we can attack stress instead of sitting back, waiting for it to attack us. We can plan to make changes in our lives that will increase our joy by decreasing our stress.

When I first started thinking about this book— before any words were ever put on paper—I knew I wanted to make it very, very practical. Stress is a problem that so many people feel on a daily basis, so I wanted to make sure I offered real-life solutions that you can put into action each day. This chapter is no exception. It's one thing to talk about the importance of taking action...but it's another thing to actually put a plan into place and then execute that plan. So I want to help you do just that over the next few pages—let's make a plan together!

The following suggestions are simple actions that have scriptural basis and practical application. It's a seven-point plan, but don't feel overwhelmed by the number of action points. You might gladly implement all seven changes or you might only adopt two or three. It's not about the number of things you can do...it's about doing *something*. With God's help, you can customize an action plan for your life and begin decreasing your stress immediately.

1. Start Your Day by Spending Time with God

Far too many people start their day in a panic— hitting the snooze button, running behind, forgetting things, and eating on the go. No wonder they feel stressed. If you'll take some time at the beginning of the day to spend time with God, it will give you a solid foundation for the rest of the day. You can actually start fighting the stresses of the day before they even have time to set in by taking time to talk to God and to study His Word.

John 10:10 tells us that Jesus came in order that we "may have and enjoy life, and have it in abundance (to the full, till it overflows)." What an amazing promise! God has given us the gift of life and He wants us to enjoy it. The very best thing you can do to enjoy your life is to have a close, personal relationship with God. But in order to get there, it begins with spending time with Him. It's really not that complicated—the more time you spend with someone, the closer you feel to them. That's true with God, too. God doesn't want to just be the button we push when we have an emergency. He wants to be your very best friend! Without

> *God doesn't want to just be the button we push when we have an emergency.*

that relationship, the truth is we will always be in an emergency. It's only with God in our lives, helping and protecting us, that we can decrease stress and enjoy life.

It's pretty amazing when you think about it—you and I get to spend as much time with God as we want. We have an open invitation to invite the Creator of the universe into our lives each day. We can begin our morning speaking to Him personally and reading His promises and instructions. If you're not already doing it, this is something you should absolutely add to your action plan.

2. Exercise

A lot of people tell me they don't have time to exercise, but I've discovered we can always make time for things that are really important. If we can make time to watch a movie on television or talk on the phone, we can plan time to exercise and take care of the bodies God has given us. When we say, "Well, I don't have time to exercise," what we really mean is, "That's not a priority for me." Well, if it hasn't been a priority for you, it's time to move exercise up the priority list, because any type of exercise—and it's important to find a type that you enjoy doing— helps lessen stress in your life.

If you want to join a gym, or if you have gym equipment at home, that's wonderful, but thankfully, gyms aren't the only places we can exercise. There are hundreds of ways to get good exercise, and many of them don't cost money, require special equipment, or sidetrack your day. I know that if I'm going to exercise, it's essential that it's something I look forward to doing, and it has to be something I can fit into my day...even my really busy days.

That's why, in addition to "traditional" exercise, it's good to keep your body active in as many small ways as possible. Maybe you can walk to a friend's house instead of driving. (If you think about it, Jesus was perhaps the greatest walker of all time. He routinely walked from Galilee to Jerusalem—a distance of about seventy miles.) You could use a push mower instead of a riding mower. If you, like many people, work at a desk or in front of a computer all day, find ways to get up every so often and get your body moving.

When you experience stress, one of the best things you can do is pretty simple: *move!* Exercise is a terrific physical solution to stress. It burns up the extra adrenaline your body is producing and gets you back to a relaxed state, which means you'll be able to spend your night sleeping instead of seething. When we mention exercise, most people cringe, but it truly is a wonderful stress reliever and health builder.

When you experience stress, one of the best things you can do is pretty simple: move! *Exercise is a terrific physical solution to stress.*

I have been working out with weights regularly for ten years, but recently I added walking every day that I possibly can, and I have been truly amazed at the mental and physical energy it has given me. When we eliminate stress—and exercise does that—we always experience more energy.

That brings me to the next item in our action plan...

3. Make Sure You're Getting Enough Sleep

The cure for a lot of the problems we deal with is getting more sleep. If you're often frustrated, if you get sick a lot, if you're weepy or on edge all the time, the first thing you may want to ask yourself is, "Am I getting the right amount of sleep each night?" If you don't get the recommended eight hours of sleep each night, your mind isn't functioning properly and your immune system is being compromised.

I think it's fascinating that God created our bodies with the ability (and the need) to shut everything off and sleep. We go into a state of repair and renewal during our sleep, and we are refreshed physically, emotionally, and mentally for the next day. Some people have difficulty sleeping and need supplements or medication, but more often than not, our lack of sleep comes from a lack of discipline. We stay up too late doing other things, and we simply don't plan enough time to sleep.

Learning how to plan your evening (including downtime) will help you sleep better. I need about three to four hours in the evening to relax before I go to bed. When I get it, I sleep very well 99.9 percent of the time. I have developed the discipline of going to sleep by 9:00 p.m. and getting up at 5:00 a.m. unless I am traveling and teaching, and that has worked well for the rest of my lifestyle. I believe it is one of the reasons I feel as good as I do and can accomplish as much as I can each day. Now, my schedule may not work for you, and I'm not suggesting you do exactly as I do, but it is important for you to establish a regular bedtime and try to get a healthy amount of sleep each night.

A lot of the people I talk to are tired, and they talk

about their need to get some rest or some time off or some time to themselves. But remember, talk alone is passive and doesn't help us improve our health. We must take action. Develop the practice of regular sleep and you will enjoy your life much more.

4. Take a Vacation

We talked in an earlier chapter about the fact that many people don't schedule vacations, and I'm convinced this is a mistake. And it's a mistake that is greatly contributing to the anxiety and frustration we often feel in our lives. No matter how busy you are or how tight the budget is, it is very important to take some time to get away from the job or the normal routine and have some fun.

Enjoying a vacation is a very active way to fight stress. It's a strategically planned and executed event that will ultimately refresh your mind and your body. You don't have to spend a lot of money or travel halfway around the world; in fact, sometimes the best vacations are "staycations," when you stay at home from work and just enjoy local activities and fun things to do in your community. Whatever you choose to do—traveling cross-country, camping, going to theme parks, staying in a fancy hotel, spending a week at home in your pajamas, taking a trip to the beach—be intentional about enjoying the time off. If at all possible, resist the urge to answer work e-mails, take calls from clients, pay bills, or do the normally stress-related events in your life. When you're on vacation...be on vacation. Don't do so much on vacation that you need a vacation to get over your vacation!

I'm a very hard-working person; I actually really enjoy it. But I know it's important that I not burn myself out. I've learned to plan for and schedule days when I do nothing that is work related. This is the healthy thing to do and, in the long run, it makes me a better and more productive worker. If I can take some days off, you can, too. Don't let the pressures of your daily life be the only thing you ever experience. Find some ways to get away from the regular routine and enjoy some new places and experiences. Vacation is more than a company benefit; it's a life benefit. Even a "vacation day" can be a huge benefit.

5. Give Yourself a Reward

You'd be surprised at the motivational and the inspirational power of simple (and even silly) rewards. There is a reason kids love rewards—they work! Treating yourself to dinner or buying the new pair of shoes you wanted after you've reached a goal may be an obvious motivational scheme, but it sure is a fun one. And there is nothing wrong with having a little fun in life. Never forget that it pleases God when you take care of yourself and enjoy the life He has given you. You are worth a reward in His eyes.

When you are setting short-term and long-term goals for your life, I think it's a good idea to also write down some appropriate rewards for yourself at the same time. This will give you something to focus on when you're struggling to complete those last minutes on the treadmill or when forcing yourself to study for that test. "Just thirty more minutes and I'll treat myself to that movie night." Make sure the rewards match the challenge—big rewards for meeting big goals and smaller perks for the smaller, daily accomplishments. Just the knowledge that you are successfully reaching your goals may be enough to motivate you, but give yourself a little reward anyway. It's a great stress-reducer.

I do what I am encouraging you to do. When I sat down to write today, I planned to write for five hours and then go out on the patio and visit with my son and a friend of his who are grilling fish and steak for our dinner. Things like this give us something to look forward to in the midst of our work.

Celebration is an important part of this. Celebrations and parties help you see what you've accomplished and prepare you for the new challenges ahead. They also let your family and friends know how important your goals are to you, and having their support is always helpful. The Word of God is full of blessings, promises, feasts, and celebrations…your life can be, too.

The Word of God is full of blessings, promises, feasts, and celebrations…your life can be, too.

6. Evaluate Your Influences

Let me ask you two important questions: (1) Who or what—the people, the books, the music, the events, the entertainment choices—is influencing your life? (2) Is that influence making your life less stressful or is it making your life more stressful? The answers to those two questions go a long way in determining the life you are going to live.

David surrounded himself with mighty men (see 2 Samuel 23). He knew that in order to be a successful warrior and leader, he needed people around him who could encourage, help, and strengthen him. You and I are no different. We need people in our lives who are going to be a benefit—people who will encourage, help, and strengthen us.

Now, there are some people and some things we encounter over the course of the day that we can't avoid. We don't get to pick our coworkers and we all face stressful situations that are not of our choosing. But a lot of the stressful people and things in our lives are of our own volition. In other words, a lot of the stress we're under is because we opened the front door and let it in. This is why it is important to, on a regular basis, evaluate who or what is helping shape your opinions, feelings, and mind-sets. Because these people and these things can either be decreasing or increasing your stress levels.

I once had a friend whom I spent a lot of time with, but she had a tendency to pout if everything didn't go just the way she wanted it to. Her personality was very difficult for me to deal with because I'm a peacemaker, so every time her mood became gloomy, I found myself feeling responsible to fix it. The only way to do that was to make sure she always got what she wanted and that left me feeling manipulated.

The relationship wasn't healthy emotionally for me and it was very stressful. I finally realized that I would need to not be so involved in her life if I wanted to decrease my stress. It wasn't an easy decision to make because I didn't want her to be angry with me, but I finally did make it. You may be in relationships that are stressful, and although you can't just walk away from all of them, if there are ones that you can eliminate, it might be wise to do so in order to decrease your stress levels.

Quite often the decisions we have to make in order to reduce our stress are not easy ones, but in the long run the benefit outweighs the difficulty.

7. Do Less, Not More

Do you have too much to do? This seems to be one of the major struggles I hear today. When I ask people how they are, about 80 percent respond, "I'm busy." Common sense tells us that God isn't going to stress us out and lead us to do more than we can. Therefore, if we're being led by God's Spirit, saying yes when He says yes and no when He says no, we should be able to accomplish what He gives us to do and walk in peace. Do you need to say no more often? We should be sure when our heart says no that our mouth isn't saying yes. Sometimes trying to keep other people happy can make us very unhappy. A person who is a people pleaser must really make sure that what they are doing is pleasing God and not just people.

if we're being led by God's Spirit, saying yes when He says yes and no when He says no, we should be able to accomplish what He gives us to do and walk in peace.

We have been given the power of the Holy Spirit to live without stress. God, however, won't honor disobedience. If He's telling us not to do something that we decide to do anyway, we'll experience the painful loss of His anointing. Grace equals ability. God gives us grace to match our call. When we do our own thing, we do it on our own. When we follow His leading, He always supplies the energy.

Remember when God promised Abraham and Sarah a child? They got ahead of God and worked out a plan of their own that ultimately produced Ishmael. Finally, Isaac came according to God's promise, but I am sure they created a lot of stress and loss of joy for themselves by not waiting on God. Ishmael's name means "man of war." Isaac's name means "laughter." We can discern from their names which child brought rest and joy and which one brought struggle and stress. Ishmael is a representation of works of the flesh, which always produce struggle and stress. Isaac, however, represents waiting for God's promise, which requires faith and always brings rest.

God wants us to burn *on*, not burn *out*! Burnout comes from physical and emotional exhaustion, especially as a result of long-term stress. Stress depletes our bodies; our immune systems become weak, and sickness—even depression—can set in. Burnout causes you to be "out of control" and no longer producing good fruit. Ignoring God's instruction causes burnout. You can't overwork your mind, emotions, or your body and not eventually pay the price for excess. Whose pace are you moving at? Is it the pace God has set for you or someone else's pace? Are you stressed out from trying to keep up with everyone else? Are you a people pleaser who makes others happy at the expense of your own peace? Do you worry a lot? There was a time in my life when most of these things were problems for me, but thankfully, I finally saw that I could make changes.

I believe we can live stress-free in a stressful world, but it will require some decisions—possibly some radical decisions. Allow God's Spirit to lead you out of a stressful lifestyle and into one of peace and joy.

Things to Remember:

➤ It's important to take action in life. Sitting back and passively wishing stress would go away won't work. Ask God to help you make a plan and then aggressively put that plan into action.

➤ You can actually start fighting the stresses of the day before they even have time to set in by taking time to talk to God and to read His Word.

➤ Exercise—one of the best forms of stress-relief possible—doesn't have to be expensive or grueling. Find a physical activity you enjoy doing and work it into your schedule on a regular basis.

➤ If you're often frustrated, if you get sick a lot, if you're weepy or on edge all the time, if you are tense and easily angered or frustrated, the first thing you may want to ask yourself is, "Am I getting the right amount of sleep each night?"

➤ A vacation is a strategically planned and executed event that will ultimately refresh your mind and your body.

➤ Rewards help you celebrate what you've accomplished and prepare for the new challenges ahead.

➤ Who or what is helping shape your opinions, feelings, and mind-sets? These people, and these things, can either be decreasing or increasing your stress levels.

➤ God wants us to burn *on*, not burn *out*!

KEEP
CALM
AND
SEE THINGS
DIFFERENTLY

SIMPLE WAYS TO DE-STRESS:

✓ Make a list of things you're thankful for
✓ Drink more water
✓ Take the afternoon off
✓ Slow down
✓ Block stressful people from your Facebook newsfeed
✓ Reevaluate your calendar
✓ Get organized
✓ Think about something pleasant
✓ Forgive yourself
✓ Smile more
✓ Finish one project before starting another
✓ Do something you enjoy

CHAPTER 13

Seeing Things Differently

Calmness is the cradle of power.
—J. G. Holland

A person's perspective about a situation generally changes when they begin to see or understand something they hadn't known before. A new vantage point often produces a new attitude:

- A fussy child in a movie theater might annoy you, but when you learn the little girl has special needs, your perspective changes…and you become more patient.
- You could be aggravated with the rude barista who is messing up your coffee, but when you're told her husband filed for divorce earlier that morning, your perspective changes…and you take time to try to encourage her.
- You may be angry with your friend who hasn't wanted to meet you for your usual breakfast and coffee in over two weeks, but when she explains she's changed her diet because she's

training to run a marathon, you have new
understanding.

As you can see, new information gives us a new
perspective. And just like these examples, a new perspective is exactly what we need when dealing with
stress. So, let me give you two thoughts to consider
that will, hopefully, bring you to a new perspective:

Thought #1: The dictionary describes *stress* as
"mental, emotional or physical tension; strain,
distress." I'd add to that: "feeling pressured or
upset." It's a condition that most of us are all too
familiar with. It's a normal part of everyday life,
and none of us can get through a day without
being confronted by it in one way or another.
We live in a fast-paced world that places more
demands on us with each passing year. People
are hurrying everywhere, and they're often rude
and short-tempered. Many people are experiencing financial stress, marital stress, and the stress
of raising children. There's mental stress on the
job and perhaps physical stress caused from overwork. Many times this stressful lifestyle causes
health problems, only adding to the stress.

So, to recap Thought #1: Stress is everywhere, we
all experience it, it can provoke us to behave unwisely,

and it contributes to health problems. Now let's consider Thought #2.

> **Thought #2:** Stress is not unique to this generation, this culture, or even this time in history. Every culture group in history has dealt with stress—relationally, financially, mentally, and emotionally. The Word of God is full of stories about people who faced incredibly trying times. They fought wars, faced persecution, endured famines, and many other things.

As believers, this should cause us to look to the men and women in the Bible to see how they handled stress so we can learn from their example. Think about this...

  □ How did Daniel face the lions without panicking and screaming out in terror?
  □ How did Moses stand before Pharaoh without suffering an anxiety attack?
  □ How could Ruth remain so calm when her husband died and she had nowhere to go?
  □ How could Paul preach the Gospel in the face of tremendous opposition without being overcome with stress?

What I just described to you are some of the most stressful situations possible, but these men and women of the Bible were bold, confident, and never gave in to stress. I am sure they felt it, but they learned how to manage it.

So what is the difference between you and me, who regularly give in to the stress we see in Thought #1, and the men and women of the Bible, who confidently overcame stress in Thought #2?

Perspective! It's all about perspective.

Our perspective, up to this point, has often been that we have to handle this stress on our own—we have to fix the problem; we have to find a way to remove those things that stress us. But this self-reliant perspective only makes things worse. Our bodies were created by God to withstand a certain amount of stress, but when we push ourselves beyond that limit, we begin to experience problems.

I personally know two pastors who had vibrant, growing ministries. They were anointed by God and were helping thousands of people find and grow in their relationship with God. But they pushed themselves too hard for too long, and both of these amazing men had complete physical and emotional breakdowns. One of them, although better, still has physical problems due to the long-term stress on his body. The other man has recovered but will need to take certain medications all of his life due to the damage caused by stress.

We might wonder how this could happen to these

anointed men of God. They were working hard in ministry and their desire was to help people, but they pushed themselves too far.

Many people today are living in a perpetual state of overload—literally on the verge of collapse. A doctor once told me that I had pushed my personal accelerator to the floor and it was stuck there. When we continue stretching ourselves to the limit, like a rubber band, one day we snap.

But the men and women in the Bible we just talked about—Daniel, Moses, Ruth, Paul—they had a different perspective. They knew they couldn't handle the situation before them in their own strength, so they depended on God. They looked to the Lord, trusting that He would give them the strength, courage, and wisdom they needed.

> They looked to the Lord, trusting that He would give them the strength, courage, and wisdom they needed.

They didn't doubt God would come through for them, and it was this confidence (this perspective) that gave them the ability to step over stress as they began to walk out their destiny.

I was involved in a situation just this morning that I can share to show how looking at a problem in a different light can prevent stress. I was in the car with someone and they missed their exit on the highway, and that caused them to become disoriented and get lost for a short while. Obviously, this took time and the person driving got very upset that he had made the mistake. His emotional outburst caused even more confusion and he was obviously stressed out from the situation.

At one time in my life, I would have reacted exactly the way the driver did, but I felt no stress at all because I have learned that once we miss an exit or make a wrong turn, getting upset about it does no good at all. I also believe that all things work together for good if we trust God, and who knows, but perhaps we were saved from an accident through what we thought was a problem. The driver and I had two different perspectives on the situation. One opened the door for stress and the other closed the door to it.

In the World, but Not of the World

It is true that stress is all around us, but the good news is that, as Christians, although we may be *in* the world, according to John 17:14–16, we are not *of* the world. We don't have to operate by the world's system, reacting like the world. Our attitude and approach can be entirely different. The world responds to difficulties by being frustrated and upset, but Jesus said in John 14:27:

*Peace I leave with you; My [own] peace I now give and bequeath to you. Not as the world gives do I give to you. Do not let your hearts be troubled, neither let them be afraid. [**Stop allowing yourselves to be agitated and disturbed; and do not permit yourselves to be fearful and intimidated and cowardly and unsettled**]* (emphasis added).

This verse indicates that we need a change of perspective. I've noticed that the right mind-set and the right attitude can completely turn a situation around. If I approach something in dread, I'm setting myself up for misery before I even begin because dread creates stress. But if I refuse to dread or have a negative outlook, I open the door for God to work supernaturally and help me. I can choose my own perspective.

> The right mind-set and the right attitude can completely turn a situation around.

Jesus didn't promise that we'd never have to deal with stressful situations. In John 16:33, He said:

In the world you have tribulation and trials and distress and frustration; but be of good cheer [take courage; be confident, certain, undaunted]! For I have overcome the world. [I have deprived it of power to harm you and have conquered it for you.]

This verse teaches us that we don't have to react to stress the way the world does. Because Jesus has deprived the world of its power to harm us, we should be able to approach the challenges we face in life with a new perspective—in a calm and confident manner.

Luke 10:19 says, "Behold! I have given you authority and power to trample upon serpents and scorpions, and [physical and mental strength and ability] over all the power that the enemy [possesses]; and nothing shall in any way harm you." Here Jesus is telling us that He has equipped us to overcome the world's ways. Even though we'll be faced with challenging and stressful situations that won't always be easy to handle, He assures us that nothing can defeat us if we handle things the right way—His way! We are the only ones who can make decisions for ourselves about how we will handle the situations that arise in our lives. Life is not likely to get any easier, but our approach to life can change and that will make it easier. One of my goals in life is to stay calm no matter what happens. I have not arrived, but I am pressing on!

One morning last week I was trying to make coffee in a new coffee machine my son bought me, and I poured the coffee beans into the grinder without having a part attached that needed to be. I had to dump the beans out, and in order to do so, I had to turn the pot upside down. This may not sound like a big deal, but this particular coffee machine is large and quite heavy. When I started to dump the beans, I failed to realize the reservoir was also filled with water and that came pouring out along with the beans—the end result was a huge mess! I said, "Wonderful," and proceeded to clean it up. I was quite pleased when I had finished the cleanup and realized that I didn't feel even one tiny bit of stress or frustration from the situation. I simply dealt with it! It is so refreshing to be able to deal with things like that now and not lose my peace and get stressed out.

The same freedom can be yours if you will begin to see things differently and start practicing holding your peace instead of exploding when stressful situations come up.

Let the Holy Spirit Be Your Guide

An important factor in enjoying a peaceful, stress-reduced life is learning to be obedient to the Lord. When you follow the Holy Spirit, He will always lead you into peace. Always remember that God will never lead you into stress, because He is the Prince of Peace. God is never going to stress us out and force us to do more than we can do; however, we often do this ourselves.

We need to be sure that we're not overextending

We can learn to say yes when God says yes and no when He says no.

ourselves by trying to do too many things we *want* to do, whether it's part of God's plan for us or not. If we're doing something God hasn't approved, He's under no obligation to give us energy to do it. I believe one of the major reasons many people are stressed and burned out is because they're going their own way instead of following God's plan. We need to follow the leading of the Spirit as to what we're to be involved in and where we're to expend our energy. We can learn to say yes when God says yes and no when He says no. When we're obedient to His leading, we'll be able to accomplish what He gives us to do and walk in peace.

Learn to recognize the symptoms of stress when they first show up in you, and instead of making excuses, ask God to help you deal with it properly. If that means not doing something you would like to do, then follow God's peace and wisdom, and you will benefit by not having the draining effects of stress. I have learned a great deal in my journey with God, and one of the most important things is that *God is always right!*

Honestly, we aren't really that capable of running our own lives and doing a good job. That's why Jesus sent the Holy Spirit to lead, guide, and direct us. Romans 7:6 says we are to be led by the "prompting" of the Spirit. I can remember numerous times when I was tired and the Holy Spirit prompted me to rest, but I continued to push myself to go out or to have company. Then I ended up exhausted, instead of just being tired. As you know, exhausted people usually get grouchy and impatient. This often caused strife in our home, leading to even more stress. If I had been obedient to the prompting of the Holy Spirit, the entire problem could have been avoided. Obedience is exalting Jesus above our own natural, selfish desires. *Are you exhausted... or is Jesus exalted?* I really believe obedience is the key to victorious, healthy, happy, and peaceful living.

Bend but Don't Break

Another important lesson I've learned is to "bend so I will not break." The Bible says, "Readily adjust yourself to [people, things] and...if possible, as far as it depends on you, live at peace with everyone" (Romans 12:16–18). Before I made the Word of God a priority in my life and decided to live an obedient life, I had to have my own way; otherwise I got upset. I wasn't adaptable. I wanted everyone else to adapt to me. Of course, that resulted in more strife and stress. I've now learned to bend. It's not always easy on the flesh to give in and do things differently than I had planned, but it's easier than being upset and miserable.

A prompting is a "knowing" down inside of you that lets you know what you should do. The prophet Elijah referred to it as a "still, small voice" (see 1 Kings 19:12). While you may not hear an audible voice, I believe you can sense God's wisdom giving you direction in certain situations.

I remember one time when I'd been shopping for several hours and was getting very tired. I had only purchased about half of the items I intended to buy, so I kept pressing on. The prompting of the Spirit within me was telling me to stop and go home, but because I hadn't accomplished my goal, I didn't. Although the other things I intended to get weren't immediate needs, I didn't want to leave until I had accomplished the goal I had set for myself. As I pushed myself beyond the point of being tired, it became difficult for me to think clearly. I then began to become impatient with other people. Even after I finally went home, I was out of sorts, and it affected my time with my family.

If I had obeyed the prompting of the Spirit and gone home to rest and relieve the stress, I would have felt so much better, and the situation at home would've been much more pleasant. We can avoid many stressful situations simply by obeying the Holy Spirit's prompting.

Burnout comes from physical and emotional exhaustion, especially as a result of long-term stress.

Burnout comes from physical and emotional exhaustion, especially as a result of long-term stress. When stress depletes our bodies, our immune systems become weak and sickness (even depression) can set in. Signs of burnout include extreme fatigue, headaches, insomnia, gastrointestinal problems, and tension. Other manifestations may also be extreme tension or an inability to relax—and when you go to the doctor he can't find anything wrong. Emotional exhaustion (crying easily), anger, negativity, irritability, depression, cynicism, and bitterness about the blessings of others can also be part of burnout syndrome. Burnout causes you to feel "out of control" and no longer producing good fruit. Ignoring God's laws causes burnout. You can't overwork your mind, emotions, or body and not eventually pay the price.

I want to urge you to take some time at this point to honestly evaluate your life and how you feel most of the time. Whose pace are you moving at? Are you keeping the pace God has set for you or someone else's? Are you stressed out from trying to keep up with everyone else? Are you living under the stress of competition and comparison? Are you a perfectionist with unrealistic goals? Do you carry a false sense of responsibility and burden yourself with problems that are not even yours? Or perhaps you are just addicted to constant activity and don't even know how to stop. It seems that most of us really hate to admit that we just cannot do it all, but once we do, life gets much easier and manageable.

I believe we can live stress-free in a stressful world, but it'll require some decisions—possibly radical ones. Allow God's Spirit to lead you out of a stressful lifestyle and into one of peace and joy. Respect your body. Treat good health and feeling good as a valuable gift. Don't waste the energy God has given you on stress. Save it for living and enjoying life. Here are some wise instructions from God's Word to make the practice of peace a part of your everyday life:

> *Don't waste the energy God has given you on stress. Save it for living and enjoying life.*

First of all... *Be still!* Stop all the rushing around. Psalm 46:10 says, "Be still, and know...that I am God." The Creator of the universe wants a word with you, but how can you hear Him if you're always on the go? Learn to listen!

Second... *Prepare your heart* to receive from Him—to hear His voice on a regular basis. "Oh, that they had such a [mind and] heart in them always [reverently] to fear Me and keep all My commandments, that it might go well with them and with their children forever!" (Deuteronomy 5:29). Can you hear the earnestness in God's voice as He makes that statement?

Finally...*Acknowledge Him* in everything you do. Make it a lifestyle to be identified with Jesus Christ and faithfully be a doer of the Word. "And the peace of God, which passeth all understanding, shall keep your hearts and minds through Christ Jesus" (Philippians 4:7 KJV).

If you'll make the choice to begin changing the way you see things, it's amazing how quickly it will change your life. When you "live in the world but not of the world," "let the Holy Spirit be your guide," and "bend but don't break," you are setting yourself up to live with the strength and confidence we saw in those men and women of the Bible who refused to give in to stress.

We would be wise to follow the example of these biblical heroes and adopt their perspective. We sometimes get so focused on our daily problems that we lose sight of God's divine purpose. Regardless of how difficult your boss is, how frustrating the leaky faucet is, how low the bank account sinks... God has a great plan for your life. The difficulty you are facing doesn't

> *We sometimes get so focused on our daily problems that we lose sight of God's divine purpose.*

change that. If you'll take time each day to get a proper perspective and trust God's plan for your life, the little things that try to bring stress into your life won't seem so important anymore.

Things to Remember:

➤ New information gives us a new perspective—and a new perspective is exactly what we need many times (especially when dealing with stress).

➤ Stress is not unique to this generation, this culture, or even this time in history. Every culture group in history has dealt with stress.

➤ The men and women in the Bible—like Daniel, Moses, Ruth, Paul—they had a different perspective. They knew they couldn't handle the situation before them in their own strength, so they depended fully on God.

➤ An important factor in enjoying a peaceful, stress-reduced life is learning to be obedient to the Lord. When you follow the leading of the Holy Spirit, He will always lead you into peace. Remember... God is always right!

➤ Because Jesus has deprived the world of its power to harm us, we should be able to approach the challenges we face in life with a new perspective—in a calm and confident manner.

➤ If you'll make the choice to begin seeing things from God's viewpoint, it's amazing how quickly it will change your life.

Did you know?

Just thirty minutes of walking per day can help boost mood and reduce stress levels.[1]

KEEP
CALM
AND
BLESS OTHERS

CHAPTER 14

The Quickest Way to Defeat Stress

You have not lived today until you have done
something for someone who can never repay you.
—John Bunyan

A story is told that during some of the darkest days
of World War II, England was running low on coal
and needed to dramatically increase its production:

> Winston Churchill called together all the coun-
> try's labor leaders in order to let them know of
> the situation and to hopefully gain their sup-
> port. At the end of his presentation, Churchill
> asked them to picture in their minds a parade
> that he knew would be held in London's famed
> Piccadilly Circus after the war.
>
> First, Churchill said, would come the sailors
> who fought to keep the vital sea-lanes open.
> Next would come the British soldiers who had
> come home from Dunkirk and then gone on

to defeat Rommel in Africa. Then would come the pilots who had driven the Luftwaffe out of the British skies.

Last of all, Churchill said, would come a long line of sweat-stained, soot-streaked men in miner's caps. Someone would cry from the crowd, "And where were you during the critical days of our struggle?" And from ten thousand throats would come the answer, "We were deep in the earth with our faces to the coal."[1]

Something powerful happens when you serve others—when you don't think of yourself, but you put the needs of others before your own. As this story illustrates, not all jobs are prominent. Not every person can fight on the front lines. But sometimes the most important people are the ones who serve (and many times, they are the happiest, too). They don't always get recognized. They may not always get the credit they deserve. But the people with their "faces to the coal" don't usually need the applause of others, because they have found something far more rewarding—the joy and deep satisfaction of helping others.

Obsession with self is a breeding ground for stress, pressure, and anxiety.

I've discovered that this is a vital key in reducing stress in our lives. As long as we are focused on ourselves—*our* problems, *our* concerns, *our* wants, *our* needs—stress attaches itself to all those thoughts. Obsession with self is a breeding ground for stress, pressure, and anxiety. But the moment we put the needs of another ahead of our own, stress begins to fade away. It's nearly impossible to bless somebody else and worry about yourself at the same time. So, if you want a tried-and-true method to reduce the stress in your life…take a look around you and find someone to bless.

In Order to Love Others, You Must First…

Love always requires action. It's not just a *thing* we try to get for ourselves, but instead it is an *action* we express to others through doing something, like sharing and serving. Love is much more than a word, or a theory—it is an action. I believe there are three very important directions God gives us concerning who to show love to.

#1: *Loving God*

Deuteronomy 6:5 says, "And you shall love the Lord your God with all your [mind and] heart and with your entire being and with all your might." In the New Testament, Jesus repeats this command and even points it out as the most important commandment of all (as well as loving your neighbor as yourself). (See Matthew 22:37–39.)

Many people ask me, "Joyce, how do I express my love to God?" Is it by telling Him, 'I love You, God'? Is it by singing worship songs to Him? Is it by going to church?" These are all good things and when done out of a sincere heart, they definitely display love for God. We show God we love Him through our relationship with Him. We want to spend time with those whom we love, so it stands to reason that loving God will display itself in wanting to spend time with Him. I like the thought of "doing life with God"—including Him in everything we do and talking with Him throughout each day. Being obedient to God's will is one of the highest forms of showing love for Him. Jesus said, "If you love Me, you will obey Me" (see John 14:15). I believe our level of obedience grows as we get to know and experience His love, goodness, and faithfulness in our lives. Our desire to follow and obey the Lord's commandments increases as we increase our love of God.

Forty years ago, I would have said I loved God if I had been asked, but I was only somewhat obedient, so I obviously loved God only to a certain degree. As the years have gone by and I have fallen more deeply in love with Him, I have also become more obedient to Him. The two go hand in hand. I suspect I will be growing like this all of my life and so will you.

#2: Loving Yourself

It is interesting to note that when Jesus talked about the greatest commandment of all, He quoted Deuteronomy 6:5 and said we are to love God with all our heart. But many people forget that He also added the second greatest commandment: "You shall love your neighbor as yourself" (see Mark 12:31).

There's something important here that I think people often miss: *You cannot give away something you don't have in you.* How can you or I love someone else if we don't even know how to love ourselves? This is why God wants us to accept ourselves, embrace our personalities and even our imperfections, knowing that although we are not where we *need* to be, we are making progress. Jesus died for us because we have weaknesses and imperfections, and we don't have to reject ourselves because of them. God wants you to love yourself and enjoy how He's made you! This is often very difficult for people to do, but it is important. God loved us enough to send Jesus to die for us, and we need to receive His love and have a healthy love for ourselves. Appreciate the fact that you are formed and fashioned by God for a special purpose and accept yourself.

> You cannot give away something you don't have in you.

#3: Loving Others

> *We know that we have passed over out of death into Life by the fact that we love the brethren (our fellow Christians). He who does not love abides (remains, is held and kept continually) in [spiritual] death.*
>
> 1 John 3:14

This is exciting to see: *Life,* in this verse, is the life of God or *life as God has it.* That's God's promise to us! We don't have to go through life as people who live and breathe but never truly live as God desires. We want to enjoy all God has for us! And the best way to do that is by serving, helping, and blessing others. When you do that, God pours out His abundant life in return! Anne Frank said it this way: "No one has ever become poor by giving."[2]

Loving others is the only way to keep the God-kind of life flowing through you. God's love is a gift to us; it's in us, but we need to release it to others through words and actions. Left dormant, it will stagnate like a pool of water with no outlet. The act of helping others is one of the most exhilarating things I have experienced. I feel excitement stirring in my

I feel excitement stirring in my spirit and soul when I plan to do something to make someone else feel loved and cared for.

spirit and soul when I plan to do something to make someone else feel loved and cared for.

You can experience the same exhilaration just by "loving out loud." In other words, let love be loud in your life. Do it often and aggressively. Here's a challenge: Think of three people you know who could really use a gesture of God's love. Then think of creative ways you can express His love to these people (if you get stuck, I'll give you some suggestions in a moment). Now go out and do it. I guarantee you will feel a wonderful sense of fulfillment and joy afterward. Now, try that same thing every day. You may think that you don't have time, but showing love takes only a few moments. It can be as simple as a smile, a compliment, or a genuine concern for those who are hurting.

If you will devote yourself to loving God, loving yourself, and loving others, you will experience a huge amount of blessings in your life. I encourage you to seek God about this and ask the Holy Spirit to help you grow in these three areas. He will help you overcome anything that might hinder you in the process. Remember, God *is* love. He loves you. And He wants you to share that love with others.

This Is Something I Had to Learn

I did it all wrong for years. And I was stressed beyond belief! I'm talking about my attitude that was focused on the thought *What about me?* And it came out in my behavior: If I didn't get my way or if I was disappointed in an outcome, I just couldn't let it go. I was constantly upset and frustrated. Frankly, I wasn't very fun to be around.

I honestly didn't know why I was so unhappy and frustrated until God spoke to my heart one day and said, "You're selfish. You've studied My Word about spiritual warfare, faith, healing, how to succeed, having power and authority as a believer in Christ… but how much time have you spent studying about My love?"

That was the beginning of discovering that I would never be happy and have peace until I learned to love others and serve them like Jesus. One of the first messages God put on my heart to teach was titled "Tell Them I Love Them." At first, I didn't want to do it. I thought people already knew that. But God showed me that if people really knew He loved them and what that means, then they would live much differently than they do.

And here is the great thing: When we know and experience God's love, we can share it with others. Imagine what the world would be like if everyone who calls themselves a Christian would really help one another and share God's love. Think about it. There would be no gossip, no judgment or criticism, no exclusive attitudes that make others feel rejected, and people's needs would be met much more than they are.

Thankfully, Jesus gave us very real, practical examples of how we can love the way God loves us. John 13:1 says Jesus "loved them to the last and to the highest degree." In the following verses, He demonstrates what it means to love others like this. And it shocked the disciples. In those days, there were servants who washed people's feet when they came to visit. It's likely they were considered the lowliest servants in the household. Now Jesus, the Son of God Himself, got up from supper, took the servant's towel, and proceeded to wash the disciples' feet. His message to them was to love one another by serving others, because God wants His love to flow through us and touch other people's lives. That means there should be nothing we think we are too good to do. In whatever manner God prompts you to serve someone, gladly do it. You never know how your act of obedience and service might affect them . . . and you.

Love is not just a feeling or a theory; it's a decision we make and an action we take. It's important for us to study what the Bible teaches about God's love so we can learn to love like Jesus. And we have to pray for God to help us learn how to walk in love—to be a servant who "washes feet"

> *Love is not just a feeling or a theory; it's a decision we make and an action we take.*

by helping others. Ask for creative ideas concerning a variety of ways that you can show your love to others.

Treat Others the Way You Want to Be Treated

Matthew 7:12 (NIV) says, "So in everything, do to others what you would have them do to you." This is critical because if we want to have healthy, joy-filled relationships with others, then we need to invest in their lives by giving them support, encouraging them, helping to meet their needs—serving them as we're able to do it.

It's easy to want to help people you like or those you want to impress. But when it comes to doing something for someone you don't know or someone you don't have a natural interest in, it can be more challenging. I also want to encourage you to be sure that you show love for and are willing to help and bless the members of your own family. Sometimes in our effort to help others, we may forget those who are of our own household. Family is very important!

I want to encourage you to read John 13 and pay close attention to what Jesus did and what He said. Spend some time studying Scriptures about God's love and pray for Him to show you ways you can serve the people in your life. See how many creative ways God puts in your heart to "wash feet." You'll probably find it's easier and simpler than you thought it would be to help make someone's life better.

God wants us to have success and enjoy our lives. In order to truly do that, we will need to be unselfish and begin each day ready to help anyone God places in our path who is in need. When you do this, you'll discover you're actually more satisfied, content, peaceful, and happy than you've ever been in your life.

How You Can Serve, Help, and Bless Others

I asked you earlier to pray and ask God to show you some ways to serve others—after all, prayer is the most important thing you can do. I want to help you in this process, too. So I've put together a list of simple suggestions of ways you can serve, help, and bless people you know... and even people you don't:

- Take someone out for lunch.
- Ask someone about a short-term goal and help them meet it.
- If you have a friend who needs to talk, take her out and listen. Just listen.
- Mow a neighbor's lawn who is out of town or ill.
- Leave a kind note for a coworker you don't normally get along with.

- Befriend someone at a party who looks out of place.
- Let someone go before you in line at the grocery store.
- When someone does something well, make sure you tell others about their success.
- Surprise a family you know by making them dinner and bringing it to their home.
- Look around your home and see if there are things that you could give to someone who has less than you.
- If someone asks you for a favor…do two favors.
- Be generous when you tip a server at a restaurant.
- Volunteer in your community.
- When a friend tells you how busy he is, ask if there is anything you can do to lighten his workload.
- Do your spouse's least favorite household chore for them.
- Send flowers to a friend "just because."

This list is just the beginning—we could probably fill an entire book with ways to serve, help, and bless others. I encourage you to pray about this list and see if God speaks to your heart about any of the things suggested here. If a friend's name came to mind, and

if you see a way to bless that person in the list above...
go for it! Stress will be the last thing on your mind.
You'll be too excited about being a blessing.

Don't Be a Martyr

We all know what a martyr is. We've all heard heroic
stories of brave individuals who, down through the
ages, have paid the ultimate price and been killed for
what they believe. But there's another kind of martyr
who's not quite as brave. I'm sure we all know one—
a great and constant sufferer who's always willing to
share his or her pain with anyone who will listen.
These martyrs want everyone around to feel sorry
for them, loudly sharing the sacrifices they're making in their lives.

I once knew a woman like this. She felt like a slave
to her family, and she definitely had the attitude of
a martyr. I have to admit, I got pretty tired of hearing her continually talk about how much she did for
everyone and how little anyone appreciated her. I
could tell she kept a running account of the work she
was doing and comparing her work to the rewards
she was (or was not) receiving for it. Eventually, she
ruined her marriage and most of her relationships
with her children. What a tragedy!

The "martyr trap" is such an easy one to fall into.
We may even start out serving our families and

friends and loving it. But after a while, our hearts begin to change and we begin to *expect* something in return. After all, we're working so hard and sacrificing so much. Eventually, we no longer have the heart of a servant. We become discouraged because our expectations aren't being met. Our attitudes sour, and we soon find out we've become mired in self-pity. We've become martyrs.

Let me tell you a little story of how this attitude can creep into our lives. Here is what happened with me...

One morning as I got up and went downstairs to make my coffee, the Lord encouraged me to make a fruit salad for my husband. Dave loves fruit salad in the morning, and I knew it would be a nice gesture for me to do this for him. He wasn't up yet, so I had time to prepare it and then surprise him with it when he came downstairs.

The problem was I didn't *want* to make him a fruit salad. I would've taken him a banana or an apple, but I didn't want to take the time to cut up all the fruit, put it in a bowl, and then serve it to him. I wanted to go pray and read my Bible instead! I thought, *Why should I do that for him; he doesn't bring me my breakfast! After all, I have to study the Bible and pray in order to teach God's Word. It's my ministry!*

Quite often when I am praying, I ask God to show me ways I can be a blessing to Dave, and yet when

He answered my prayer, I didn't want to follow His advice. Praying to be a blessing sounds spiritual and loving, but we should make sure we intend to follow through when God shows us what to do.

The fruit salad is such a little thing that it may not even seem worth mentioning, but I believe it is often the little things that we don't do that cause some of the biggest problems in our relationships.

It's funny how we sometimes make the mistake of thinking that spiritual activity is better than a simple act of kindness. The Lord patiently reminded me that serving my husband in this way was actually serving Him. So I obediently made the fruit salad and surprised Dave with it when he came downstairs.

Although Dave didn't pay me back or go overboard in his appreciation, I found a joy in knowing I had obeyed God and in just being a blessing to my husband.

I wonder how much stress in marriages would be reduced if husbands and wives would be willing to show love by simply serving each other. Why not try it? Ask God to show you little things you can do to serve your spouse and then do them and watch how your spouse's attitude toward you improves as time goes by.

> I wonder how much stress in marriages would be reduced if husbands and wives would be willing to show love by simply serving each other.

I definitely love my husband, and sometimes that love is best expressed through service. Words are wonderful, but when you walk in love, your commitment must contain much more than just words. How can I truly love my husband if I never want to do anything for him? I don't recall getting any particular reward that morning for making Dave's fruit salad. He did thank me, but nothing spectacular happened. However, I'm sure there were rewards of peace and joy in my life that I didn't even realize—benefits of obedience that I didn't even see. I'm convinced we lose a lot of blessings we never even know about simply because we fail to do for others what we would like to have done for us, or we do things for people and yet we do it with a wrong attitude—the attitude of a martyr. Let's do what we do for others without expecting anything in return, and then we will have the joy of receiving God's reward in due time.

If your marriage or family isn't what you would like it to be, you could literally turn it around by adopting this one principle right now. You may have been waiting for your spouse to do something for you. Maybe you have even been stubbornly refusing to be the first to make a move. Swallow your pride and save your marriage. Stop talking about all the sacrifices you make and start serving with a right heart attitude. Make *them* the focus, not you...and be a servant, not a martyr.

Ask for Nothing Except to Serve

As we finish this chapter, I want to share a story with you that demonstrates the value of serving and helping another...

Franklin Roosevelt's closest adviser during much of his presidency was a man named Harry Hopkins. During World War II, when his influence with Roosevelt was at its peak, Hopkins held no official cabinet position. Moreover, Hopkins's closeness to Roosevelt caused many to regard him as a shadowy, sinister figure. As a result, he was a major political liability to the president. A political foe once asked Roosevelt, "Why do you keep Hopkins so close to you? You surely realize that people distrust him and resent his influence." Roosevelt replied, "Someday you may well be sitting here where I am now as president of the United States. And when you are, you'll be looking at that door over there and knowing that practically everybody who walks through it wants something out of you. You'll learn what a lonely job this is, and you'll discover the need for somebody like Harry Hopkins, who asks for nothing except to serve you." Winston Churchill rated Hopkins as one of the half dozen most powerful men in the world in the early 1940s. And the sole source of Hopkins's power was his willingness to serve.[3]

Just like the source of Harry Hopkins's power was

his willingness to serve, there is power in your life for serving others. And when you do it, the results can be life changing. Joy is restored, peace reigns, stress is lowered, and God is pleased. So even though the demands in your life seem pressing today, I want to encourage you to put some of those things on the back burner and turn your attention to others. Look for ways to encourage; look for ways to bless. And you know what? When all is said and done, you might be surprised to find that you were the one who was encouraged and blessed more than anyone else.

You may be wondering why stress would be reduced if you took time to serve others. Won't that just add to the myriad of things you already have to do? The amazing thing is that the more we have our minds on ourselves, the more stressful it becomes, but when we forget ourselves for a while and focus on what we can do for others, we find a joyful relief we may not have been expecting.

Things to Remember:

➤ Something powerful happens when you serve others—when you don't think of yourself, but you put the needs of others before your own.

➤ As long as we are focused on ourselves—*our* problems, *our* concerns, *our* wants, *our* needs— stress attaches itself to all those thoughts.

➤ Loving others is the only way to keep the God-kind of life flowing through you. God's love is a gift to us; it's in us, but we need to release it to others through words and actions.

➤ "So in everything, do to others what you would have them do to you" Matthew 7:12 (NIV).

➤ When you make a list of ways to serve others, stress will be the last thing on your mind. You'll be too excited about being a blessing.

Did you know?

Stressed is "desserts" spelled backward.

KEEP
CALM
AND
START FRESH

CHAPTER 15

The First Day of the Rest of Your Life

A contented mind is the greatest blessing a man can enjoy in this world.

—Joseph Addison

One of the wonderful things about God is that He loves new beginnings. With God, you don't have to live in the bondage and pain of yesterday; you can live in the beauty and promise of tomorrow. That's why Scripture promises that God's compassion and mercies are "new every morning" (see Lamentations 3:23). God doesn't just allow "do-overs"; He created them! Consider the stories we read about in the Word of God:

- Moses killed an Egyptian and ran from his destiny...but God gave him a new beginning as the deliverer of His people.
- David was a shepherd boy who was slighted by his own father...but God gave him a new beginning as the king of Israel.

- Gideon was afraid of the enemy and hiding in a wine press...but God gave him a new beginning as a mighty military leader.
- Peter was hot-tempered and denied he even knew Christ...but God gave him a new beginning as the leader of the early church.
- Paul persecuted Christians and stood by as Stephen was stoned...but God gave him a new beginning as an apostle, a missionary, and author of most of the New Testament.
- Mary of Magdala was filled with demons and yet she became one of Jesus' close friends and traveling companions.

Do you see the trend? No matter what the personal struggle or failure, God forgives, heals, restores, and makes things new. He's been doing it since man first sinned, and He's still doing it today.

And you know what? God wants to do it for you, too—He wants to give you a new start. Regardless of the pain, the pressure, the anxiety, or the stress you've been living with, God wants to give you a brand-new start. He wants to take all that away and give you a new freedom in Him. In 2 Corinthians 5:17 you'll find this promise:

Regardless of the pain, the pressure, the anxiety, or the stress you've been living with, God wants to give you a brand-new start.

Therefore if any person is [ingrafted] in Christ (the Messiah) he is a new creation (a new creature altogether); the old [previous moral and spiritual condition] has passed away. **Behold, the fresh and new has come!** (emphasis added)

That's good news—the fresh and new have come! Stress, anxiety, worry, and pressure are the old things that you had learned to live with...but God is making all things new. You don't have to live that way anymore. Today, tomorrow, and every day forward can be a new start. You can live full of peace and overflowing with joy. Today isn't just another day when you are stressed out and overwhelmed—today can be the first day of the rest of your new life!

Now, there are going to be times when the old stresses and anxieties come knocking on your door. In the pages of this book, you learned how to kick them out of your life, but that doesn't mean they won't try to sneak back in. So in this last chapter, I want to give you some final tools for your spiritual toolbox that will help you live a peaceful, joy-filled life from this day forward.

Choosing to live with joy doesn't mean that we never experience any negative emotions like anger, sadness, or disappointment. It does mean that we have a choice not to let them rule us. Most of the emotions that we experience in life are very normal and even necessary. How could I be qualified to minister to you about your emotions if I had never experienced anything but good ones? All of our experiences in life are what form us into the people that we are. But once again, I want to stress that we can choose to let our emotions rule our behavior or to manage them in such a way that, although we don't deny their existence, we do deny them the right to control us.

The following recommendations are helpful suggestions that will aid you in remaining stable and enjoying your life.

Choose to Live with Hope

How do you generally feel about your future? Do you have hope that good things will happen? Or do you generally feel stressed, expecting negative or disappointing things to happen?

I was taught to be negative when I was growing up. I lived in an abusive atmosphere with negative people, alcoholism, fear, and anger. As a result, I developed an attitude that it was better to expect nothing good than to expect something good and be disappointed when it didn't happen. Sadly, I often wondered, *What's going to go wrong next?*

It wasn't until I was an adult that I realized I was living with negative expectations, which created a vague feeling around me all the time that something bad was going to happen. Then one day, God spoke to my heart about this. He showed me that I was dreading that something bad was going to happen, but He wanted me to expect good things to happen. Jeremiah 29:11 tells us that God's thoughts and plans for us are "for welfare and peace and not for evil, to give you hope in your final outcome." God wanted me to joyfully believe and even say out loud, "Something good is going to happen!"

He wants you to do that also. Expecting good and living with a positive attitude are great stress reliev-

> God doesn't work in us through negative attitudes of any kind.

ers. God is good, and as we walk with Him and learn His ways, we can expect more and more good things to come to us and flow through us to other hurting people. Negative expectation always equals pressure and that means stress. The truth is, God doesn't work in us through negative attitudes of any kind. Whether it is worry, anxiety, self-pity, jealousy, laziness, or unforgiveness—these are not peace-producing attitudes. God works through faith! But in order to have faith, it is essential that we first have hope. Faith and hope go together—you can't have one without the other. Hope is a favorable and confident expectation; it's an expectant attitude that something good is going to happen and things will work out, no matter what situation we're facing. Zechariah 9:12 says:

> *Return to the stronghold [of security and prosperity], you **prisoners of hope**; even today do I declare that I will restore double your former prosperity to you* (emphasis added).

I really like the phrase *prisoners of hope*. Think about it: If you're a prisoner of hope, you have no choice about it—you can't be negative. And when times are tough, and you're dealing with disappointment or you're feeling stress creep in, hope will cause you to rise up in faith and say, "God, I praise You and I believe You're working on this situation and working in me. My faith, trust, and hope are in You!" Believe that God *is* working, and avoid thinking that God *will* work at some time in the future. Faith is always "now," and it is what we believe now that affects the life we are living now!

Hope is determined to see God's best and it never gives up. God wants us to expectantly trust that He can change what needs to be changed, that we can accomplish what He has called us to do, and that His promises are going to come true in our lives. If we will be steadfast in our hope, we can't lose—we are destined to succeed with God's help. I can tell you for sure that our enemy, Satan, is always working to steal hope from us. He is the source of all the temptation we experience to be hopeless, anxious, and stressed out in life. But the truth is that we already have the victory as long as we apply God's wonderful principles to our lives, trusting in Him at all times.

There will be tough days. Don't assume that everything will get better the minute you put this book down. (Human nature is impatient, selfish, and wants things quickly. Why is it that although it takes us years to get into our messes, we expect God to get us out of them in a few days?) In John 16:33, Jesus tells us that we are going to have tribulation, trials, distress, and frustration in this world, but in spite of that, we can be of good cheer and take heart. Why? Because He has overcome the world. And when we live in Him, we become overcomers, too! That's why Jesus died for us. He came to save us from sin and death and to give us abundant life—*now*.

I am determined to have everything Jesus died to give me. I encourage you to make that same decision— be determined to receive and enjoy every good thing Jesus died to give you. You'll have to do it on purpose. But you can be determined to do what God wants you to do and refuse to live with negative expectations. Ask God to help you live in hope and declare by faith, "Something good is going to happen to me!"

Press on...Even When It's Difficult

An important part of battling stress and worry is making right choices while you are hurting, discouraged, frustrated, confused, or under pressure—even though the right choice is often the harder choice. When you're in the middle of terrible stress, you naturally want to take the path of least resistance. Those are the very moments when you can make a conscious effort to make the tougher choice. To reap right results in life, you must decide to do right when you don't feel like it. I call this "pressing in and pressing on"—and knowing how to do it is one of the most important components of being a person who doesn't live as a victim of stress.

Any kind of progress in life requires effort. Being a person who makes major life changes will require an investment on your part. You'll only get to where you want to be by willingly sacrificing and pushing through the obstacles or adversities that stand in your way. But you can be assured that sacrifice always eventually brings a reward. Your obstacle might be a habit of giving in to stressful situations— in the past, you may have simply lived as a victim of your environment, allowing the circumstances to determine your mood. Whatever it is, you are the only one who can press through it; no one else can do that for you. I believe it is time for you to take charge of your life and follow God's will instead of bowing down to pressure that is designed to prevent you from living out your destiny.

Maybe you tried to make some changes in the past. Perhaps you tried to the point that you are now weary, exhausted, or discouraged. If so, then you are at the precise point where you need to summon fresh strength from God and press in one more time. Many times we grow weary, and we falter in our determination if we do not continually lean on God, trusting in His strength rather than our own strength. We can make the decision to press through, but we never experience success in anything unless we rely on God to help us. His grace is always sufficient to enable us to do what we need to do.

When we put our hope and dependence in God, He'll give us the strength we need. Don't wait to feel the strength before you step out in faith! We never have to wonder if He'll come through. If we will keep moving forward, even when things get difficult, God will always show up and do what we could not do on our own. The Word of God says it this way:

But those who wait for the Lord [who expect, look for, and hope in Him] shall change and renew their strength and power; they shall lift their wings

and mount up [close to God] as eagles [mount up
to the sun]; they shall run and not be weary, they
shall walk and not faint or become tired.

Isaiah 40:31

One of the definitions I've heard for the word *press* is "to exert steady force or pressure against something." That's why I often say, "You have to press against the pressure that's pressing against you!" When something is pressing against you, you can be determined to press against it with greater force, because very little that is truly worthwhile or worth having in life happens without this kind of effort. And remember, you're not pressing against stress in your own strength; you have the strength of the Holy Spirit. "He Who lives in you is greater (mightier) than he who is in the world" (1 John 4:4).

Sometimes you have to press through stressful circumstances to overcome obstacles, such as when your dream is to open a business in a certain neighborhood but the zoning board repeatedly rejects your request to build the facility you need, or when your dream is to go to college, but you keep getting turned down every time you apply for a scholarship. I suffered sexual, mental, and emotional abuse as a child. Because of this, I needed to move away from home and begin supporting myself immediately after high school. My high school teachers recognized a writing gift in me and strongly urged me to try for a college scholarship, but I did not get to go to college. Obviously, that didn't stop God! I've written more than one hundred books and I never had formal training to learn how to do it. I have also received several honorary degrees and have earned two degrees because of my writing. I could not go to college the so-called normal way, but God had another way to help me do what He wanted me to do. I am amazed when I think of what God will do if we simply decide to press in...even when it's difficult. Another way to say it is: Never give up!

Tough situations and challenges in life must be dealt with, but I am more concerned about your response to the obstacles than about the obstacles themselves. If you can keep your thoughts and attitudes right—and if you will refuse to let stress defeat you through trusting God—you will eventually have the breakthrough you need. I can't promise you will get exactly what you want, but if God doesn't give you what you are asking for, then He will give you something much better. His ways and thoughts are above ours (see Isaiah 55:9).

Think about your life and make a fresh determination to pay the price of progress. As you face the obstacles in your life, remember: Press in and press on.

Focus on How Far You've Come Already

Let me tell you about a conversation I had with a friend we'll call "Cheryl"...

Cheryl told me, "Joyce, I've been a Christian for twenty-three years, and I'm just not getting anywhere. I'm as weak as I was when I first accepted Christ as my Savior. I still fail. I just don't know if it's worth it." She was very discouraged and tears kept running down her cheeks as she talked about her mistakes and shortcomings. She went on to say, "By now I know all the right things to do, but I don't do them. Sometimes I deliberately do something mean-spirited or unkind. What kind of Christian am I?"

I answered her very matter-of-factly: "Probably a growing Christian. If you weren't growing, you wouldn't be sad about your failures. You'd be satisfied about your spiritual level and not concerned with growing." She said, "But, Joyce, I still fail so often!"

I went on to tell Cheryl she was correct that she had failed. All of us do at times. None of us are perfect. If we're not careful, we can focus only on what we haven't accomplished and where we have been weak and never see the progress we have made. When that happens, it's easy to feel bad or want to give up. That's not the way God works. No matter how many mistakes we make, God doesn't give up on us. The Spirit continues to work with us and make us more like Christ.

My advice to Cheryl, and to all Christians who face those dark moments, is to look at all *God* had done in her life rather than seeing all *she* had yet to do. Yes, life is sometimes a struggle, and there are times when we fail and make mistakes. We don't ever reach the place where we never have a struggle or a temptation. But here is the key thing to remember: God sent Jesus because we are weak at times and we need His help and forgiveness. Jesus is not only with you, but He is also *for* you. He knows your heart's desire is to do

> Jesus is not only with you, but He is also for you.

better. He knows where you came from, but He also knows where you are headed and He will never give up on you!

My friend kept remembering the times she had failed, but I reminded her of the times she had succeeded. "You think you're losing, but that's not true. You have failed at times, but you have also succeeded. You have stood your ground and you have made progress." That's the same message I have for you today. You may have gone through some trying times, you may have dealt with your share of stress, you may know what it's like to feel overwhelmed, but you're still here and you're still moving forward. With God's help, you are making progress! After all, you have almost made it to the end of this book! That is an accomplishment in itself.

Let me remind you of something the Word of God says:

> *Fear not, for I have redeemed you...I have called you by your name; you are Mine. When you pass through the waters, I will be with you, and through the rivers, they will not overwhelm you. When you walk through the fire, you will not be burned or scorched, nor will the flame kindle upon you.*
>
> Isaiah 43:1–2

This is God's promise. He never said that He will take us completely out of troubles or hardships, but He does promise to be with us as we go through them. Anytime you are *going through*, you are still making progress because you have not given up! "Fear not," He says. That's the message we need to remember. We don't need to fear because God is with us. And when God is with us, what is there to be stressed about? He's already brought you this far...just imagine how far He is going to take you in the future.

Never Give Up

Galatians 6:9 says, "And let us not lose heart and grow weary and faint in acting nobly and doing right, for in due time and at the appointed season we shall reap, if we do not loosen and relax our courage and faint."

In this scripture, the apostle Paul is simply encouraging us to keep on keeping on! Don't be a quitter! Don't have that old "give up" spirit. God's looking for people who will be courageous and keep moving forward in Him. Even at times when progress seems slow, remember that any progress is better than going backward.

For many years I felt I was making very little, if any, progress in my spiritual growth and overcoming bad habits and behaviors. But now as I look back, it is amazing how different I am, and the same thing is happening and will continue happening to you.

Whatever you may be facing or experiencing in your life right now, I want to encourage you to stay positive and refuse to go back to those anxious, worried, stress-filled mind-sets. God *is* with you. He'll help you experience His peace and joy—strengthening and encouraging you to keep on keeping on during rough times. It's easy to quit (anyone can do it), but it takes faith to press on to victory.

When the battle seems endless and you think

you'll never make it, remember that you're reprogramming a "worldly" mind to think as God thinks. Your mind may be like a computer that has a lifetime of bad information programmed into it. But God— the best "computer programmer" around—is working on us every day to reprogram our minds as we cooperate with Him (see Romans 12:2). This process of reprogramming or renewing our minds will take place little by little, so get excited about your progress, even if it seems slow.

It is not God's will for you to be overloaded and stressed out about anything. Jesus came to give us peace and we can learn to live peacefully in the midst of turmoil and enjoy our lives while God is solving our problems.

Things to Remember:

➤ With God, you don't have to live in the bondage and pain of yesterday; you can live in the beauty and promise of tomorrow. God loves new beginnings!

➤ Regardless of the pain, the pressure, the anxiety, or the stress you've been living with, God wants to give you a brand-new start.

➤ God's thoughts and plans for us are "for welfare and peace and not for evil, to give you hope in your final outcome" (Jeremiah 29:11). Knowing this is a key to living with hope.

➤ If we'll wait patiently, pressing in even when things get difficult, God will always show up and do what we could not do on our own.

➤ Look at all *God* has done in your life rather than seeing all *you* have yet to do.

➤ Whatever you may be facing or experiencing in your life right now, stay positive and refuse to go back to those anxious, worried, stress-filled mind-sets. It's easy to quit (anyone can do it), but it takes faith to press on to victory.

SIMPLE WAYS TO DE-STRESS:

- ✓ Take a nap
- ✓ Enjoy a delicious, nutritious meal
- ✓ Do something special for yourself
- ✓ Make a list of your strengths
- ✓ Volunteer to do something that will help someone else
- ✓ Count your blessings
- ✓ Call a friend who has a way of encouraging you
- ✓ Play with your dog (if you don't have a dog, play with your neighbor's dog)
- ✓ Get outdoors for a while
- ✓ Cut back on your caffeine intake
- ✓ Eat less sugar
- ✓ Turn off your electronics for an hour
- ✓ Read uplifting material
- ✓ Smile for no reason in particular

NOTES

Chapter 1: Start Defeating Stress Today

1 "Stressed Out: Americans Tell Us About Stress in Their Lives," http://www.npr.org/blogs/health/2014/07/07/327322187/ stressed-out-americans-tell-us-about-stress-in-their-lives.

2 *2013 Work Stress Survey* conducted by Harris Interactive on behalf of Everest College, http://globenewswire.com/news -release/2013/04/09/536945/10027728/en/Workplace -Stress-on-the-Rise-with-83-of-Americans-Frazzled-by-Some thing-at-Work.html.

3 "Who's Feeling Stressed? Young Adults, New Survey Shows," http://www.usatoday.com/story/news/nation/2013/02/06/ stress-psychology-millennials-depression/1878295/.

4 http://apa.org/news/press/releases/stress/2014/highlights.aspx.

5 "Who's Feeling Stressed? Young Adults, New Survey Shows," http://www.usatoday.com/story/news/nation/2013/02/06/ stress-psychology-millennials-depression/1878295/.

6 "Stress Management," http://www.mayoclinic.org/healthy -living/stress-management/in-depth/stress-symptoms/art -20050987?pg=1.

7 "Fact Sheet on Stress," http://www.nimh.nih.gov/health/pub lications/stress/index.shtml.

8 http://www.heartmath.com/blog/health-well-being/what -you-need-to-know-about-stress/.

Chapter 2: Who's in Charge?

1 http://www.rd.com/health/wellness/37-stress-management
   -tips/3/.

Chapter 3: The Best Stress-Relief Possible

1 Compiled from the following sources: H. R. Beech, L. E.
   Burns and B. F. Sheffield. *A Behavioural Approach to the Management of Stress*, ed. Cary L. Cooper and S. V. Kasl (Chich-
   ester: John Wiley & Sons, 1982), 8, 9, and 11; Randall R.
   Cottrell, "The Human Stress Response," in *Grolier Wellness
   Encyclopedia: Stress Management*, 1st ed, vol. 13 (Guilford:
   Dushkin Publishing Group, 1992), 34, 35; *Webster's II*, s.v.
   "adrenal gland," "endocrine gland," "pituitary gland."
2 Tim Hansel, *Holy Sweat* (Word Books Publisher, 1987), 46–47.
3 Lawrence Chilnick. *Heart Disease: An Essential Guide for the
   Newly Diagnosed* (Philadelphia, PA: Perseus Books Group,
   2008). Facts.randomhistory.com/stress-facts.html. Accessed
   April 22, 2015.

Chapter 4: I'd Like to Exchange This

1 http://www.quotegarden.com/stress.html.

Chapter 5: Decisions You Make and Steps You Take

1 http://www.goodreads.com/quotes/tag/inner-peace.
2 Jennifer Warner, "Stress Makes Teen Acne Worse." WebMD
   .com. March 7, 2002. Facts.randomhistory.com/stress-facts
   .html. Accessed July 5, 2015.

Chapter 6: Did You Forget Something?

1 "Benefit." *American Dictionary of the English Language 1828*.
   1995.

2 Lawrence Chilnick, *Heart Disease: An Essential Guide for the Newly Diagnosed* (Philadelphia, PA: Perseus Books Group, 2008). Facts.randomhistory.com/stress-facts.html. Accessed April 22, 2015.

Chapter 7: Choice Overload

1 http://www.nytimes.com/2010/02/27/your-money/27shortcuts.html.
2 http://www.economist.com/node/17723028.
3 Ibid.
4 http://www.brainyquote.com/quotes/quotes/h/henrydavid166869.html.
5 Gene Wallenstein, *Mind, Stress, and Emotion: The New Science of Mood.* (Boston, MA: Commonwealth Press, 2003). Facts.randomhistory.com/stress-facts.html. Accessed April 22, 2015.

Chapter 8: Laugh, Laugh, and Laugh Some More

1 http://www.marketwatch.com/story/americans-only-take-half-of-their-paid-vacation-2014-04-03.
2 http://www.mayoclinic.org/healthy-lifestyle/stress-management/in-depth/stress-relief/art-20044456?pg=1.
3 Ibid.
4 http://www.brainyquote.com/quotes/quotes/c/charliecha108932.html?src=t_laughter.

Chapter 9: The Stress of Comparison

1 http://www.nytimes.com/2011/07/02/your-money/02shortcuts.html?_r=0.
2 http://www.sermoncentral.com/illustrations/sermon-illustration-robert-leroe-quotes-envy-82561.asp.

3 http://www.sermonillustrations.com/a-z/e/envy.htm.

4 http://sermonquotes.com/post/101193685702/comparison -is-the-thief-of-joy-theodore.

5 http://www.ncbi.nlm.nih.gov/pubmed/1534428.

Chapter 10: Change the Conversation

1 Gene Wallenstein. *Mind, Stress, and Emotions: The New Science of Mood* (Boston, MA: Commonwealth Press, 2003). Facts.randomhistory.com/stress-facts.html. Accessed July 5, 2015.

Chapter 11: It Is Well with My Soul

1 http://www.spaffordcenter.org/history and http://www.share faith.com/guide/Christian-Music/hymns-the-songs-and-the -stories/it-is-well-with-my-soul-the-song-and-the-story.html.

2 Bruce McEwen, *The End of Stress as We Know It* (Washington, DC: Joseph Henry Press, 2003). Facts.randomhistory.com/ stress-facts.html. Accessed April 22, 2015.

Chapter 13: Seeing Things Differently

1 http://www.nimh.nih.gov/health/publications/stress/index .shtml.

Chapter 14: The Quickest Way to Defeat Stress

1 http://www.sermonillustrations.com/a-z/s/service.htm.

2 http://www.goodreads.com/quotes/tag/helping-others.

3 http://www.sermonillustrations.com/a-z/s/service.htm.

Do you have a real relationship with Jesus?

God loves you! He created you to be a special, unique, one-of-a-kind individual, and He has a specific purpose and plan for your life. And through a personal relationship with your Creator—God—you can discover a way of life that will truly satisfy your soul.

No matter who you are, what you've done, or where you are in your life right now, God's love and grace are greater than your sin—your mistakes. Jesus willingly gave His life so you can receive forgiveness from God and have new life in Him. He's just waiting for you to invite Him to be your Savior and Lord.

If you are ready to commit your life to Jesus and follow Him, all you have to do is ask Him to forgive your sins and give you a fresh start in the life you are meant to live. Begin by praying this prayer...

> *Lord Jesus, thank You for giving Your life for me and forgiving me of my sins so I can have a personal relationship with You. I am sincerely sorry for the mistakes I've made, and I know I need You to help me live right.*
>
> *Your Word says in Romans 10:9, "If you declare with your mouth, 'Jesus is Lord,' and believe in your heart that God raised him from the dead, you will be saved" (NIV). I believe You are the Son of God and confess You as my Savior and Lord. Take me just as I am, and work in my heart, making me the person You want me to be. I want to live for You, Jesus, and I am so grateful that You are giving me a fresh start in my new life with You today.*
>
> *I love You, Jesus!*

It's so amazing to know that God loves us so much! He wants to have a deep, intimate relationship with us that grows every day as we spend time with Him in prayer and Bible study. And we want to encourage you in your new life in Christ.

Please visit joycemeyer.org/salvation to request Joyce's book *A New Way of Living*, which is our gift to you. We also have other free resources online to help you take your next steps in pursuing everything God has for you.

Congratulations on your fresh start in your life in Christ! We hope to hear from you soon.

ABOUT THE AUTHOR

Joyce Meyer is one of the world's leading practical Bible teachers. Her daily broadcast, *Enjoying Everyday Life*, airs on hundreds of television networks and radio stations worldwide.

Joyce has written more than one hundred inspirational books. Her bestsellers include *Power Thoughts*; *The Confident Woman*; *Look Great, Feel Great*; *Starting Your Day Right*; *Ending Your Day Right*; *Approval Addiction*; *How to Hear from God*; *Beauty for Ashes*; and *Battlefield of the Mind*.

Joyce travels extensively, holding conferences throughout the year and speaking to thousands around the world.

JOYCE MEYER MINISTRIES U.S. & FOREIGN OFFICE ADDRESSES

Joyce Meyer Ministries
P.O. Box 655
Fenton, MO 63026
USA
(636) 349-0303

Joyce Meyer Ministries—Canada
P.O. Box 7700
Vancouver, BC V6B 4E2
Canada
(800) 868-1002

Joyce Meyer Ministries—Australia
Locked Bag 77
Mansfield Delivery Centre
Queensland 4122
Australia
(07) 3349 1200

Joyce Meyer Ministries—England
P.O. Box 1549
Windsor SL4 1GT
United Kingdom
01753 831102

Joyce Meyer Ministries—South Africa
P.O. Box 5
Cape Town 8000
South Africa
(27) 21-701-1056

JOYCE MEYER SPANISH TITLES

Belleza en Lugar de Cenizas (Beauty for Ashes)
Buena Salud, Buena Vida (Good Health, Good Life)
*Cambia Tus Palabras, Cambia Tu Vida (Change Your Words, Change
Your Life)*
El Campo de Batalla de la Mente (Battlefield of the Mind)
*Como Formar Buenos Habitos y Romper Malos Habitos (Making Good
Habits, Breaking Bad Habits)*
La Conexión de la Mente (The Mind Connection)
Dios No Está Enojado Contigo (God Is Not Mad at You)
La Dosis de Aprobación (The Approval Fix)
Empezando Tu Día Bien (Starting Your Day Right)
*Hazte Un Favor a Ti Mismo...Perdona (Do Yourself a
Favor...Forgive)*
Madre Segura de sí Misma (The Confident Mom)
Pensamientos de Poder (Power Thoughts)
Termina Bien tu Día (Ending Your Day Right)
Usted Puede Comenzar de Nuevo (You Can Begin Again)
Viva Valientemente (Living Courageously)

* Study Guide available for this title

BOOKS BY DAVE MEYER

Life Lines